Ameri-Sicula:
Sicilian Culture in America

Praise for *Ameri-Sicula: Sicilian Culture in America*

"In his new book, Mark Hehl presents several wonderful recollections by Sicilian-Americans of their families and their Sicilian culture. The stories recount the families' transition from Sicilian to America life, and their struggles and successes. In each story the writer, in his own and unique way, tells of his connection to, as one writer puts it - "family, food and faith" - and especially food! Anyone of Sicilian heritage will truly appreciate this collection of family remembrances. Indeed, any Italian-American will be able to relate to the experiences of these enjoyable stories - as I did."

Salvatore DiPillo

Mark Hehl has accomplished a true labor of love of our Sicilian heritage in this absorbing collection of poignant stories and family lore. Many of the tales introduce customs and phrases that were new to me, while many, even from *"paisi stranii" (other villages),* bring sweet memories of the feelings, aromas, tastes, shouts and laughter that are fondly remembered from my youth."

Angelo F. Coniglio, author of *The Lady of the Wheel (La Ruotaia)*

"Mark Hehl's anthology of stories from the Sicilian diaspora centers around the collective history of Sicilian Americans growing up with their extended immigrant Sicilian families, and dovetails seamlessly with my many happy memories growing up with my father's extended Sicilian family in a small suburb of Pittsburgh, PA. What explains the magnetic pull Sicily exerts on her expat sons and daughters? I didn't fully understand myself until I starting traveling back to Sicily in the mid-1990s and experienced firsthand the beauty and mystery of the island. Beauty, because Sicily is like a glimmering jewel placed in the palm of your hand; and mystery because virtually every Sicilian family has a story of heartbreak – the heartbreak of a people departing this magical island and the family they left behind."

Betsy Vincent Hoffman, author of *Dreaming of Sicily: A Travel Memoir*

Ameri-Sicula:

Sicilian Culture in America

Edited by
Mark Hehl

Ameri-Sicula: Sicilian Culture in America, edited by Mark Hehl

ISBN 978-1-939693-40-2
Library of Congress Control Number: 2020942746

Acknowledgements:

First and foremost, I thank the contributing authors who have responded to my call and spent the time and effort to submit their chapters. Hopefully, their work will help to preserve our traditions for generations to come.

I am grateful to Dr. Gaetano Cipolla of *Arba Sicula* and *Legas* for his dedication to Sicily, support, and assistance with this book.

As with my other books, my wife Olga has been instrumental with improving my grammar and editing the manuscript. Her efforts resulted in a well-written and fine- tuned literary piece.

I thank Lauren Sequenzia for assisting me with the technical aspects in formatting this book.

My gratitude goes to my sister, Valerie, for keeping the Sicilian Christmas Eve celebrations going for years after our mother passed.

By giving me six grandchildren, my children: Erik, Devon and Lauren provided me with the motivation to embark on this book project so that my descendants and other future generations will appreciate the Sicilian-American experience.

The publisher is grateful to Carlo Puleo for the use of his painting entitled "L'archivio dei ricordi," published in *La Pittura*, Palermo: Thule, 1998.

The publisher is grateful also to Arba Sicula for its generous grant that in part made the pubblication of this book possible.

For information and for orders, write to:

Legas

P.O. Box 149
Mineola, New York
11501, USA

3 Wood Aster Bay
Ottawa, Ontario
K2R 1D3 Canada

legaspublishing.com

To my grandchildren
Jake, Nellie, Kaila, Alex, Louis, and Lacey

Ameri-Sicula: Sicilian Culture in America
Mark Hehl, Editor and Author
Contributors

Joseph L Cacibauda
Louisa Calio
Bill Cimino
Gaetano Cipolla, Ph.D.
Anthony J DeBlasi
Rosemary DeMaio Fairel
Hank Ferraioli
Claudio Finizio
Marisa Frasca
Devon Hehl
Erik Hehl
Joanne Cantarella Ingargiola
Salvatore Liotta
Anthony Malatino
Josie Marino
Constance Miceli, DSW / Ph.D.
Serafino Pace
Michael D Pasquale, Ph.D.
Tony Patti, Esq.
Nino Provenzano
Richard Rotella, M.D.
Allison Scola
Lauren Sequenzia
Mario Toglia
Mafalda LaCruba Tornello
Alfred Zappala, Esq.

Table of Contents

PART II
From Our Island

PART III
Our Language

PART IV
Our Cuisine

Preface

Like many other Sicilian–Americans my age, I grew up with a foot in two worlds. At home, my mother maintained many rich Sicilian traditions. In school, and on the streets of Brooklyn, I was American.

My first years were spent in a close-knit Sicilian neighborhood on Halsey Street in the Bushwick section of Brooklyn, NY. Most of the residents were from a few Sicilian towns, including a large population from my ancestral village of Santa Margherita di Belice (AG). I am fortunate to have these memories, being the oldest surviving sibling/cousin and probably the only one to remember this. I grew up surrounded by grandparents, aunts, uncles, cousins and even one great-grandmother, who did not speak English. I remember her saying to me and my cousins at meals "Mancia e zittiti!" (eat and shut up).

Sunday family gatherings were at Uncle Eddy's (born Ignacio) house, across the street from where I lived. We needed to walk through the basement to reach the yard, as gatherings were outside when the weather was good. At my uncle's house, I played with my cousins and ate authentic Sicilian food. Eggplant, figs, tomatoes, sausages, and pasta were usually on the menu. The vegetables were homegrown. My memory of eating caponata was resurrected during my visits to Sicily. Caponata is an eggplant-caper based salad that the Arabs brought to Sicily during their reign there. When tasting it while in Sicily, I said to my wife: "This tastes like Brooklyn." My childhood memories just hit me like a thunderbolt.

Being engrossed in marriage, children and a professional career caused me to almost forget and not practice these wonderful childhood traditions. Soon after writing my second book An Immigrant's Dilemma, Legas Publishing, Mineola, NY, I realized that the Sicilian–American traditions that I was exposed to were not passed down to my children. I suspect that my failure was not unique and that others of my generation were also deficient at this. This provided me with the motivation to document some of these traditions I remember and solicit contributions from other Sicilian–Americans. This way, these rich traditions would not be lost and could be passed down to future generations.

The following pages are the results of this work.

Introduction

I conceptualized this book as a compilation of traditions of Sicilian immigrants and their descendants. As responses to my call for contributors were received, the scope of this book was expanded. Being that from 1816-1861, Sicily and Southern Italy were united as Regnu dî Dui Sicili (The Kingdom of the Two Sicilies) I included some chapters from other southern Italian traditions, as these traditions are similar to the Sicilian experience.

Stories about food, language and life in Sicily were submitted and were included. It services to enhance this work.

I kept the various writing styles of the individual authors. Hopefully, this should provide variety and pleasurable reading.

PART I

Our Traditions and Memories

"The family occupies the most prominent place in the lives of Sicilians. The family is the single most important institution around which revolve the social behaviors of Sicilians. It's a symbol of the unity of the Sicilian people as a nation, and it is a means of defense against outsiders. For Sicilians one could really say the family is all. Each member of the family unit has precise responsibilities and duties from the father as the head, the mother as the emotional center and the children owing allegiance to their parents and their siblings. This is evident in the love that adults bestow on children. They are protective of them to obsessive measures."

Reprinted by permission from the book: *What Makes a Sicilian?*, Gaetano Cipolla, Legas, 1996

Chapter 1

My Wonderful Sicilian-American Childhood

Mark Hehl

The special food, my extended family and hearing broken English on Sunday afternoons is still fresh in my mind after more than 60 years. Some of these flavors were absent from my memory until I visited Sicily as an older adult and re-experienced them. These are my childhood memories growing up Sicilian-American.

My first years were spent in a close-knit Sicilian neighborhood on Halsey Street in the Bushwick section of Brooklyn, NY. Most of the residents were from a few Sicilian towns, including a large population from my ancestral village of Santa Margherita di Belice (AG). I am fortunate to have these memories, being the oldest surviving sibling / cousin and probably the only one to remember this. I grew up surrounded by grandparents, aunts, uncles, cousins and even one great-grandmother, who did not speak English.

Sunday family gatherings were at Uncle Eddie's (born Ignacio) house, across the street from where I lived. His house was an attached dwelling. We needed to walk through the basement to reach the yard, as gatherings were outside when the weather was good. At my uncle's house, I played with my cousins and ate authentic Sicilian food. Eggplant, figs, tomatoes, sausages and pasta were usually on the menu. The vegetables were homegrown. My memory of eating caponata was resurrected during my 2007 visit to Sicily. Caponata is an eggplant-caper based salad that the Arabs brought to Sicily during their reign there. When tasting it, I said to my wife: "This tastes like Brooklyn." My childhood memories just hit me like a thunderbolt.

Unfortunately, these gatherings came to an end when most of my relatives moved to Queens-Nassau county border. My family was the only one to stay in Brooklyn; we moved to the Cypress Hills section (a mixed ethnic neighborhood), when I was five years old and did not rejoin the extended family until we moved to Queens-Nassau border, twelve years later.

My mother maintained the Sicilian traditions at home. On the street, playing stickball, and at school, I was American. This *foot in two worlds* helped me in my career dealing with many world cultures while working in over forty different countries. I realized that the American way was not the only nor the best way.

I remember my school lunches. My mother would cook lunch each morning. These sandwiches (peppers and eggs, veal cutlet, etc.) were olive oil-based and the other children would make fun of me saying that I had greasy or soggy sandwiches. I would come home crying. Once my mother came to school and complained to the lunch lady (Mrs. Russel) and my tormentors were subsequently scolded. Now I realize how lucky I was to have such good food while those taunting me were eating peanut butter or bologna.

After high school, I attended and graduated from three local colleges (while living in my parents' home) and would buy lunch at school. When my mother found out that I was eating hot dogs and hamburgers there, she insisted on making me lunch again as she did not think that that this "American junk food" was good enough for me. However, this time I did manage to get her to back off by promising to eat more acceptable items on the menu.

I remember her saying that she could not believe that my German-American paternal grandmother would just boil vegetables and serve them plain, without any garlic and olive oil. For my mother, food had to be flavorful. Olive oil and garlic went on most food. Eating at my paternal relatives' homes was always a disappointment. The only German food that my grandmother made that I liked was spaetzle. I even remember making it with her. This grandmother would tell people that her daughter-in-law was a very good cook.

The nuns in my Catholic grammar school used to remark that Italian food was greasy but they still ate *the most popular cuisine in the world*. Yes, olive oil is an oil but a good one and there are multiple health benefits from garlic and the Mediterranean diet.

I now have a wife who is an excellent cook. Did I get lucky! As with most life situations there is good and bad. I have and still eat well but struggle to control my weight.

The distrust of the government and police brought over from the old country was embedded in our culture. People in my neighborhood would not cooperate with the police and answer questions. "I know nothing" was a common response. People trusted only family and close friends. They were used to corrupt officials in Sicily, especially the *carabinieri* (national police) and the federal government.

Having a Non-Italian surname helped me to avoid some prejudice but not all. Growing up, I was often called a *ginzo,* an ethnic slur that I still hate to hear. I was fortunate to attend a Catholic high school and remember that the teachers (Catholic Brothers) favored the Irish-American students. This reminded me that, even in the 1960's, some people considered Italian-Americans to be second class citizens. My parents' generation was sensitive to this prejudice and did not want us to learn to speak Sicilian. They thought that not speaking the Sicilian language would help us to avoid abuse and allow us to assimilate better. I wish that my relatives would have spoken Sicilian to me so that I would now have the wonderful gift of a second language. My mother only used Sicilian when I was in trouble and I am afraid to repeat the terms she used when she was upset. It is rewarding to see that recent immigrants work to maintain their native language and pass it down to future generations. I now struggle to learn and constantly improve my Italian and Spanish language skills.

Another unfortunate result of prejudice, bigotry and ignorance was the practice of Americanizing given names. My uncle was born Ignacio but used Edward, my grandmother changed her name from Maria to Mary. Many professionals and entertainers (Dean Martin, for example) were forced to do the same to ensure success. My siblings, cousins and I were given American names. Americanizing ones' name was a common practice at that time. Fortunately, new immigrants do not follow this practice.

Another unfortunate situation was that organized crime was associated with Sicilians. These very few but very bad apples, caused the rest to suffer. I remember hearing many times "all of you *ginzos* are Mafia criminals". It was common to hear the phrase "he (she) must be connected" when someone with an Italian name got a good grade in college or a promotion at work. Some people could not accept that a successful Italian-American did well due to perseverance, determination, dedication and hard work or to put it another way, GRIT.

Reprinted from: *An Immigrant's Dilemma,* Mark Hehl, 2019, Legas.

Chapter 2

Sicilian Advent, Christmas, and Epiphany Traditions

Michael D. Pasquale, Ph.D.

Christmas has been a special time for our family since I was a child. I have carried on that love of the season but have also desired to include Sicilian and Italian cultural aspects into our celebrations. This desire is shared by my family and was enhanced when we went through the process of gaining our dual Italian citizenship a few years ago.

Our family deliberately waits to start celebrating Christmas until after Thanksgiving in the United States. This usually lines up with the church calendar and the four weeks of Advent. Our family decorates a Christmas tree and uses advent candles. One important family tradition is for us to put up our nativity set, called a presepio in Italian. Traditionally these were more common to have in Italy than a Christmas tree. Our set is particularly special since my grandmother, who was a potter, made our set by hand years ago.

The first event that we added was to celebrate St. Nicholas Day on December 6th each year. We have our children place their stockings on the mantel on the evening of December 5th in anticipation of St. Nicholas visiting. We love telling our children the story of the "real" St. Nick and his work serving the poor and caring for children. The gifts that we place in the stockings are traditional, like a bag of chocolate coins to represent the small bag of money that St. Nicholas was said to give to the needy. We also give them the traditional gift of a piece of fruit, such as a clementine or small orange. We spend some time sharing with the children how St. Nicholas Day was celebrated in Sicily. I have read that the day is considered a minor holiday now but was considered more important in years past. We have taken the time to celebrate the day with a meal featuring our favorite Sicilian food such as spaghetti in squid sauce or arancini. Traditionally in Sicily there has also been thc custom of serving St. Nicholas bread (bread with the initials "SN" baked into it). We don't have access to that bread, but we do serve panetonne cake. This cake is more Italian than Sicilian, but widely available in Italy today. One tasty traditional treat that we enjoy is the fig cookie, often called a buccellato, called cucchidati by our family.

The next important date on the calendar is December 13th, the Feast of St. Lucia. This day which honors St. Lucia is still important in Sicily today. We will usually tell the story of St. Lucia to our children and perhaps listen to a recording of the traditional "Santa Lucia" song.

Our Christmas celebration is a family affair and starts with a feast on Christmas Eve. Our extended family exchanges gifts on Christmas day and the traditional North American "Santa Claus" visits and fills our children's stockings once again. Our Christmas day dinner is rather "American" in that we often celebrate with a turkey dinner with sides such as green bean casserole. But the gathering of family around the table is distinctly Italian and includes card games such as the traditional Sicilian game Cu Cu.

While our American neighbors tend to start taking down their Christmas decorations the day after Christmas or on New Year's Day, our family continues the festivities with the Twelve Days of Christmas. The Twelve Days of Christmas are the days between Christmas and Epiphany (January 6th). The culmination of our Christmas season is another feast on the eve of Epiphany and celebrating the arrival of the Three Kings (the Magi). However, today in Italy the day also celebrates the story of La Befana, an old woman who gives gifts to children just like Saint Nicholas or Santa Claus. We spend time telling the story of the woman and her connection with the story of the Three Kings. In the traditional telling, she is approached by the Three Kings on their way to see baby Jesus and they stay at her home. They invite her to join them to see the baby Jesus, but she declines because she has too much work to do. However, she later regrets that decision and goes out to seek the Magi and tries to find baby Jesus. According to tradition, she is still searching to this day.

La Befana is traditionally represented as a witch with a broom. The name "La Befana" is thought to come from the Italian word for Epiphany "epifania." What is interesting is that as I sought to understand how my relatives celebrated Epiphany in the past a similar tradition was shared. My grandmother would talk about "Witch Tresina" who would bring oranges to the good children and sticks or stones to the bad children on the evening of Epiphany. I had wondered if there was any relation to the story of La Befana. One of the theories given for the background for La Befana is that she is based on the Roman goddess Strenia, the goddess of the new year, purification, and well-being. It is plausible that the witch "Tresina" from my grandmother's memory is related to this Roman goddess "Strenia."

We love the intentionality and process of celebration that incorporates Sicilian and Italian cultural traditions. We were able to enjoy a lengthened holiday season with multiple days of gift giving and days to enjoy tasty Sicilian treats such as cuccidati!

Chapter 3

Feast of St. Joseph

March 19
(A pamphlet published by St. Anselm Catholic Church
Madisonville, Louisiana)

by Joseph L. Cacibauda

MEMORARE TO ST. JOSEPH

Remember, O most pure spouse
Of thy
Blessed Virgin Mary,
My sweet protector, St. Joseph
That no one ever had recourse
To your protcction
Or implored your aid
Without obtaining relief.
Confiding therefore in your goodness,
I come before you
And humbly supplicate you.
O, despise not my petitions,
Foster father of our Redeemer,
But graciously receive them.
Amen

St. Joseph Feast Customs

Ceremony of the "Saints"

The Bethlehem story is reenacted at the altar. People are chosen to represent the Holy Family, favorite "saints" and "angels." Joseph seeks shelter for Mary by knocking on three doors. At the first two they are turned away, but at the third they are warmly welcomed with the words "Whatever I have is yours. Come and eat at my table."

The “saints” are then led to the altar table that is set with the finest table service. They are reverently served. Jesus opens the ceremony by cutting the bread that is to be eaten by the “saints.” St Joseph is always served first, and tradition denotes the order in which the courses are presented. With the exception of pasta, there are always three portions of the same food on each plate representing the holy Trinity and the Holy Family. Fruits begin the feast, followed by bread, Pasta Milanese with Mudica, seafood, vegetables, cookies, desserts, water, and wine. Before beginning to eat the “saints” must listen for the words “Mangiate, santos dolces” (Eat, sweet saints). At the close of the ceremony, the saints are given one of the symbolic breads. Jesus takes the cross, Mary the palm or heart and Joseph the staff or beard. The altar is then broken and all guest are invited to share in the special meal.

Blessing of the Altar

The day before the actual feast day a priest blesses the entire altar and the adornments. Visitors come that evening to pray and leave petitions and donations that are given to the poor.

Three-Tiered Altar

The altar is built in three tiers, which represent the Three Person in the Blessed Trinity. A statue of St. Joseph or a picture of the Holy Family is placed on the top tier surrounded by floral arrangements and fruit.

Fresh Green Branch

A fresh green branch is place above the door where the altar is erected as a sign of welcome and invitation to the public to share the feast.

St. Joseph’s Bread

Special breads in various symbolic shapes are blessed and distributed at the altar. They may be eaten but are often saved. During storms*, a small piece is thrown out and prayers are said in hopes that the storm will cease.

Meatless Meal

Although there is no definitive reason why meat is never served at the altar, several speculations exist. The primary reason is that the feast is celebrated during Lent and it reminds the visitor of the Last Supper.

Bags

Bags are given to the visitors of the altar as keepsakes. The bag usually contains a holy card with a picture of St. Joseph and a prayer, a fava bean, bread or cookies, and a blessed medal.

Begging

All food on the altar is obtained by begging for donations. Those who have been favored with good fortune continue to share these blessings with those in need. Donations and food for the altar are sent to the poor. There is never personal profit gained from the altar.

St. Joseph Altar Symbols
(Breads and Cakes made in the images of Christian Symbols)

(Spada) holds the Sacred Host

Chalice

Consecration of the Bread and Wine at the Last Supper

Cross

Crucifixion Of Christ

Doves

The Holy Spirit

Lamb

Jesus, the Lamb of God

Fish

Christian symbol of Jesus Christ

Bible

A large cake that is one of the focal points of the altar

Hearts

Sacred heart of Jesus, Immaculate Heart of Mary

Wreaths

Crown of thorns, also symbol of eternal love

Palms

Palm of martyrdom, also the palms cast at the feet of Jesus as he entered Jerusalem

Other Symbols in Breads and Cakes:

Lilies, ladder, sandals, staff, hammer, beard, nails, saw

Muddica

Browned and seasoned breadcrumbs sprinkled over the Pasta Milanese representing the sawdust of Joseph the carpenter.

Pinolatti

Fried pastry molded in the shape of pinecones representing the pinecones that Jesus played with as a child.

Twelve Whole Fish

Represents the 12 apostles or the miracle of the loaves and fishes.

Pupaculova

Baked bread filled with dyed eggs symbolizing the coming of Easter

Wine

Miracle of Cana

Grapes

Vineyards of Sicily

Olive Oil And Olive Salad

Olive orchards of Sicily

Dried Figs

Fig orchards of Sicily

Fava Bean

The gift of a blessed bean is the best known of the customs associated with St. Joseph's Altar. During one of Sicily's severe famines, the fava bean thrived while other crops failed. It was originally grown for animal fodder, but because of its amazing resilience, it became the sustaining food of the farmers. The dried bean is commonly called the "lucky bean." Legend has it that the person who carries a lucky bean will never be without coins. The fava bean also is a token of the St. Joseph's Altar, and a reminder to pray to St. Joseph.

The Swallows at San Juan Capistrano

The feast day of St. Joseph**, March 19th, was officially proclaimed in the 14th century. By an odd coincidence, on that date the swallows return to the California mission of San Juan Capistrano. They leave on St. John's day and have repeated this cycle for over two hundred years.

The Sicilian Legend of 101 Angels

A long time ago, a frail widow lived on the outskirts of a small village in Sicily. She was afraid, since she lived alone. But she had great faith, and every evening at dusk she prayed:

One hundred and one angels,
Watch over me and protect me,
He who comes to do me harm,
Do not give him the strength
Or the force
To open my door

One day a young man whom the lady knew from the village came to her door. He said," Signora, I have tried for three evenings to come to see you, but each time your yard was filled with many people." The widow knew immediately that the young man had intended to do her harm, for the "people" he saw had been the one hundred and one angels watching over and protecting her.

*March 19, St. Joseph's Day is also Italy's Fathers' Day and the Onomastico (name day) of Giuseppe's.

Chapter 4

My First Two Dozen Years (Extract)

Anthony J. DeBlasi

As soon as his legs and arms were strong enough, Tony walked with mama down Lorimer or Leonardz Street, or down Manhattan Avenue, to "a strada di li Giuda," the Street of the Jews. This stretch of Moore Street was packed with shops that sold their wares on the sidewalk. The goods were protected from sun and rain by retractable canvas awnings—almost the only "overhead" of the business. In this open market the shopper could meander through foodstuffs, dry goods, household wares and sundries—touch, squeeze, smell, evaluate—and bicker with the store-owner over price. Spring-loaded scales weighed what was loose. "Packaging" consisted of newspaper and paper bags. Items that could drip were wrapped in heavy waxed paper. Since the only "honest" scale was the one in mama's kitchen, protest over the accuracy of the vendor's scale could save another few cents.

If you wanted chicken, you stepped into a back-yard area where live chickens were stacked in tiers. You looked through the wooden slats of the crates and pointed to the one you wanted. The attendant grabbed the wildly clucking thing by the legs, slit its neck and thrust its head down in a metal conical holder to drain the blood into a large bucket. After a bath in piping hot water, the chicken was held against the teeth of a revolving cylinder that plucked off the feathers. It was good to get away from the smells of scalding flesh, blood and feces and get back onto the street—to shake the squawking out of his head, the sawdust off his feet.

Curb-side vendors sold snacks and drinks. Mama stopped at a cart to buy her son a knish or a sciali russu ("charlotte russe"), depending on the boy's mood. The savory fried patty of mashed potatoes and onions was a great treat. So was the spongy soft cake, topped with a frothy swirl of real whipped cream, set in a paper cup with a bottom that slid upward to bring the cake to the top. Reading Tony's face, mama sometimes stopped at a stand to order a malted milk. It excited the boy to watch the man load the goodies into the mixing container, then attach it to a whirring machine that blended the ingredients to a smooth, creamy drink that took the breath away with each gulp.

A short walk from our Johnson Avenue flat took the family to the Chiesa di Maria Santissima Rosario di Pompeii on Siegel Street. The Church of the Most Holy Mary-of-the-Rosary of Pompeii was a transplant of the Italian home-town church. Ornate but warm, it was above all a holy place. The high ceiling, the intricate spaces, the dim recesses, the lingering odor of incense, the sculpted Via Crucis panels along the side walls, dark confessionals in the rear, gilded altar in the front, life-like statues of saints with precious features peering from marble niches, the sonorous echoes of the priest's elegant Latin chant, the pure tones of trained voices in the choir loft, the penetrating, resonant sound of the pipe organ—all this stirred feelings in the boy beyond words. Here, through the glory of the weekly celebration, came direct knowledge inexpressible, yet palpable, of something vaster than the sky and the sun, the moon, and the stars. It was something unlimited by body or mind. It was God reflected in man-made objects and sounds, hinting at things unspeakable—terrifying at times—yet familiar and assuring as a mother rocking her child in calm or stormy weather. Like a mother, the church was the rock against the storms of life. Appropriately beautiful in every detail—as one would expect to find the home of a divine King—the church was where you, Creator, heritage, past, present, and future merged and focused.

Across Lorimer Street, from the corner where Tony lived, loomed a big apartment building. At each landing of a double stairwell a simple U-turn put you at the next file of stairs. (In smaller, more typical tenements the files were stacked above each other, requiring a walk to the opposite end of the stairwell for the next rise or descent.) The temptation to slide down the banisters competed with the warning not to. High ceilings amplified the sense of space. Except for the dim lighting and musty smell this could have passed for an office building with no labels on the doors. After knocking on one of them, and being loudly greeted, the visitor walked to the kitchen through a long, dim corridor. Here the DeBlasi's came to spend time with an Italian family, mixing talk with homemade wine. Tony watched the arms dance, the hands cut the air, the faces change with the speed of the words. He knew what most of the words meant. They might have been about Mussolini's victory in Abyssinia or conflict with the Vatican in Rome. The significance of the talk remained unfathomable, but the boy knew it was important stuff, judging from serious faces and passion in the voices. In time the women broke off from this faraway stuff that papa and cumpari sounded off on and talked between themselves about things closer to home and family. If cummari stopped to make coffee—always over polite protests—mama joined in the "men talk" with equal fervor. No visit was complete without a glass of homemade wine. The boy was given his glass too. The dark, potent drink filled his chest with heat on its way down to the stomach.

The DeBlasi's were occasionally invited across the hall for dinner. Mr. and Mrs. Spivak had grown-up sons and daughters and a warm heart. Yiddish and Sicilian accents spiced the conversations and it was necessary at times for the English experts to step in.

The DeBlasi boys did their best to clarify meanings. Tony took it all in, the way he took everything in, with ease. Differences in language were like differences in food. Sicilian was the official language of the house. His brothers spoke English to one another. And Italian was the language at the meetings of the Catholic Union Society. It was all quite natural.

The heat of the kitchen stove cooled on its way through the bedrooms to the parlor. The windowless inner rooms were dim even by day. Ceiling lamps cast feeble yellow light over dark furniture and wall-hangings. From a somber frame, a pious Saint Joseph holding a happy little Jesus and a stem of Madonna lilies watched over the brothers while they slept.

The youngest DeBlasi loved "maccarruna c'a sarsa." "Macaroni" were not the "elbows" of today's pasta scene. They looked like and could be used as drinking straws. It was a hearty pasta, assertive on the way down, assisted by a robust sauce: garlic and onions browned in olive oil, pureed tomatoes and tomato paste, basil, and enough sugar to correct sourness. A man's dish. The sauce was so good that Tony would not put cheese on it, for that would spoil the flavor and make the sauce pasty. He used cheese only on what he didn't care much for, to improve the flavor. The boy also loved pasta cu i piseddri. This was a dish of small-cut pasta like *tubbittuneddra* (small bead-like cylinders of equal height and diameter) cooked in a soup of tomatoes, onions and fresh peas. Pasta was always cu something—with beans, with broccoli, with what looked best to mama at the vegetable stand for the money. When the budget was extra tight, the cu was diced garlic fried in olive oil.

Past'e scarola, on the other hand, screwed the boy's face. It was the salt and olive oil in the broth, with the help of some black pepper, that gave this escarole slush permission to enter the body. No one went hungry, unless they did not eat what was served. Occasionally mama made pasta. It could be gnocchi or macaroni made by wrapping and rolling the dough around wires, then sliding the wires out before drying. This time-consuming product was reserved for feasts and holidays. Usually mama rolled the dough out on a floured board, then cut it into parallel strips, fettucini style. The pasta was then spread on a bed, on top of a bedsheet, to dry.

Parenti came to visit from time to time. Parenti were cousins, uncles, aunts—anybody however remotely related through blood or marriage. Then the kitchen hummed with soprano gossip and baritone declamation. The best plates came out and meat was served after the pasta. It was round-the-table feasting that continued into the night. It would not do for the guests to leave now. Why not stay overnight?

The sidewalks were paved with slabs of dark-gray slate. White chalk was used for drawing potsy squares and soda-cap shooting-game layouts. Numbers, letters, up-and-down lines, side-to-side lines, slant lines—it was fun even to study the patterns. It was not just chalk lines you didn't step on or stop at. You did not step on the borders between slates. God knows what might happen if you did! Boys at the other end of the block sometimes wandered over, for some fun. The leader among them thought nothing of marching the boys into an entrance, lining them up around the vestibule walls, then ordering them to show their penis. All obeyed except Tony. For this he got a stare. Group games did not appeal to him. Tony preferred one-on-one, where each guy could be himself.

The boy did not venture outdoors in winter. It was not allowed. When it was necessary to leave the house, mama wrapped him from head to toe and put a scarf around his neck. It was a blessing to have him signed into kindergarten, so that she could shop and visit in the cold without having to worry about her third son in and out of the elements. Snug at school by day and snug at home by night, the three would be safe, thank God. This fear of the cold came from dreadful experiences with respiratory infections. Though it was never mentioned, Mary would not forget the Spanish Flu epidemic that killed Papa's first wife.

Keeping warm in winter meant staying in or near the kitchen by day, conserving body heat with adequate clothing. At night, three bodies under a common blanket generated a lot of heat. The smallest boy, considered the frailest, sometimes got a hot-water bottle to bed, but his cold feet had company. Keeping warm meant buying coal for the cast-iron stove and not buying ice for the icebox. Milk was kept cold outside. With their long necks and ball-jar bottoms the milk bottles stood on the fire escape like frosty glass bowling pins. What a treat to scoop out and eat the frozen cream at the top!

Saint Barbara's cathedral was a queen among churches in Brooklyn. Its twin, white Romanesque towers formed a stately climax to a very formal Bushwick Avenue. When you entered with your class, in a file, when you took your designated seat, stood, or knelt, your attitude was that of perfect respect in the house of God. Bad manners and childish habits were left at home. Here you were to act like children of God, a relation marked with reverence, obedience, and silence. Tony knew the feeling, acquainted from birth with the power that inspires it. It was a power greater than every self and greater than everything. It was a power that inspired stained glass windows and organs and glorious music and wonderful paintings and sculptures. It was the power behind beauty and all good things. In his simple way, Tony understood that the catechism, the rosary, the praying were the formal, social means—as the Latin chant and music were the supernatural, spiritual means—of being in the grace of God.

The pain Tony felt was never from the Nun's ruler on the knuckles. He felt it whenever she stopped the lesson, opened a drawer, and took out an incredibly special cardboard box. She beamed as she removed the lid, while those who had money in their pockets—most of the children—rose from their seats and lined up at her desk to buy candy. His pocket was always empty.

Sunday dinner was sometimes simple but never trivial, the cooking typically begun on Saturday. And playing card games: Scoop or War. Or checkers. Or the piano. Weather permitting, it was most likely a visit to relatives or friends. Usually it meant a trolley ride and walk to a three-family house on Johnson Avenue. The ritual began with a call on the Piazza's, on the second floor. Cousins. Wine, coffee, cakes. Then upstairs to the Messina's. Santo's godparents. Wine, coffee, cakes. Dinner, sometimes. After a grancata (spell) at the table, men gathered in an adjoining alley to play bocci, children played hide-and-seek, and women stayed indoors and gossiped.

The Sunday outing, after dinner, was sometimes a short walk from Harmon Street to Himrod Street, to visit the Saccheri's. Wine, coffee, cakes. After sunset everyone went upstairs and sat around a radio. It was a pretty piece of furniture with four legs, dials, a tuning eye with a glowing green iris that squinted over a black background when searching stations, and a cloth grill with a loudspeaker behind it. Out of it came voices that joked and sang to the accompaniment of a band. In a voice dry as a cracker, Eddie Cantor signed off his half hour of crooning with, "I love to spend each Sunday with you." His slightly nervous voice was warmer, somehow, and more candid than the slick, ba-ba-ba-boom crooning of Bing Crosby. The teams of George Burns and Gracie Allen and Edgar Bergen and Charlie McArthy filled the little Himrod Street theater with from-the-heart-and-ribs laughter. It was obvious that without the wooden dummy, Charlie and his wooden friend, Mortimer Snurd, Bergen would not amount to beans. Likewise, without the human dummy, Gracie, Burns would be nothing.

The relationship of godparents to each other was a big deal. To be cumpari and cummari was aviri *u San Giuseppe*—"to have the Saint Joseph"—between them. Family, for Sicilians, was everything. Beloved spouse of the Virgin Mary, mother of us all, Saint Joseph was father of us all. In March, the Feast of Saint Joseph was celebrated with a table filled with fancy breads. Each design was a beautiful work of art, a shame to break and eat. The Head of the Holy Family himself would be proud to break bread together with the Ponzo's and DeBlasi's on this great feast.

Mama did not wait for feast days to cook something special. Her favorite was *cuscusu*, the Arabian dish, which she called u piattu forti dii Trapanisi, "the strong dish of the Trapanese." She sprinkled water over a thin layer of semolina on a board. With a circular motion of the hand, fingers spread spiderwise, the flour collected in small beads. These were steam-cooked in a large pot fitted over a larger pot. Meanwhile a soup of fresh cod, tomatoes, garlic, and onions simmered on another burner. When the mound of semolina kernels was ready, the hot soup was strained and poured over it and the pot covered. When the beads absorbed all the soup, the cuscusu was ready. This was flavorful, satisfying food that took most of the day to prepare and could feed an army.

Hours in the kitchen were sometimes lavished on sweets. Tony's wish for *cassateddri* was frequently granted. These deep-fried pastry sacks filled with sweetened ricotta, cinnamon, bits of chocolate and candied fruit were esteemed above cannoli. *Cassateddri* were so rich, delicious, and satisfying that they became a favorite snack while they lasted. Making them required patience, but pignulata took more than staying power. To make and fry nuggets of dough was easy, but the job of bunching them into round pyramids with boiling-hot honey was an act of skill and courage. The mounds of glossy amber nuggets, decorated with candy sprinkles, were festive on the table and crunchingly delicious in the mouth.

The Christmas holiday was inconceivable without cuddrureddri di fico. Dried figs by the pound and a lesser number of raisins went through the meat grinder, the boys taking turns at the hand crank. Ground cloves and grated orange peel—sometimes toasted and crushed almonds—were added. The mix, filling a huge aluminum pot, was softened with strong coffee. This filling was cased in pastry dough and baked to a golden brown. Unlike the soft, effeminate fig newton, these were crisp, large manly affairs. One or two could keep you to the next meal. They were good eating alone or with coffee, dry or dunked. Making them was a family enterprise. All sat around the table to roll dough, add filling, bend the elongated fig sacks into S, U or O shapes, fringe the edges with bold knife-cuts, make cuts over the tops to expose the filling, and decorate with candy sprinkles. The desire to be creative was encouraged. Rolled in one, it was art, good food, and entertainment. Laundry baskets (made by papa from soaked reeds) were filled to the brim with these Christmas *cuddrureddri*. They were given freely to friends.

While mama filled dough with figs, she filled heads with tales from old Sicily. Often it was a side-splitting adventure of Giufà, the amiable dunce who took idiomatic expressions literally ("Go jump in the lake!"). His cool-headed bungling got both him and villain in trouble. Or it was *i Vespiri Siciliani*, the spontaneous, popular uprising against the oppressive rule of the Bourbons. One evening (during Vespers) those suspected of being alien were asked to say cicira, Sicilian for chickpea. The French, who could not pronounce it right (saying something like SEE- SEE-RAH instead of SHEE-SHEE-RAH) were exposed by their own tongue. They then faced the legendary wrath of the Sicilians.

(Today's politically corrected and grossly ignorant mind needs to be told that "ethnic cleansing," highlighted in the story of *i Vespiri Siciliani*, stretches from prehistoric times to the present and across all borders, including our own. Some brother, father, uncle or other male relative or friend did just that on some battlefield in the 20th Century, whether the cause was noble or otherwise. It continues into the 21st Century in less obvious forms, such as "peace-keeping" and "regime formation," modern euphemisms for imposing the standards of the powerful over the weak. The process is active here too, not just abroad. For example, "multiculturalism" is a euphemism not for tolerance of differences but for political "ethnic cleansing" of all who do not agree with the model of a docile, compliant, amoral, globopolitan society, being pushed worldwide by moneyed elites who recognize no limit to their power. As always, and to this moment, "legitimate" political rule is the result of a (typically unequal) contest and settlement between producers and pirates. It is why in any age people enjoy seeing "the bad guy" punished by "the good guy." And why *i Vespiri Siciliani* evoked roars of laughter at the table.)

Archways with curlicue designs were raised on wooden posts over a street closed to traffic for several blocks. Bunting and lights trimmed the parade route for the feast of la Madonna di Pompeii. At twilight, the ornate arches burst into sparkling color, as their entwining lights were turned on. The smell of broiled sausages, roasted nuts, and heavenly sweets floated through the air in eddies, as curb-side vendors turned the street and sidewalks into a mile-long buffet. People thronged and milled along the chain of carts and tables, ate, drank, and gabbed in block- party fashion. Tony liked *i ciciri*, pea-sized chickpeas roasted over a fire, hissing and filling the air with a nutty odor. It was the one treat that the family could afford. Before long came a boom of drums, a splash of cymbals, a blare of brass and woodwinds from the direction of the church. *La processione* began. Musicians in white shirts played robust marches, while men in shirtsleeves carried la madonna through the streets. As the queen of all mothers passed, she was greeted with cheer and adoration and venerated with the sign-of-the-cross and prayer. When the Holy Mother returned to the front steps of her church, the sky lit up with fireworks. Brilliant streaks and bursts of light cracked the night air with volleys of artificial thunder, as gleaming cascades of color painted the sky in glorious strokes, thrilling Tony to the core. Festa—a unity of faith, family, friends, food, and fun—was to these Italians in Brooklyn as natural as breathing.

Sitting for hours on chairs around the walls of a large room—listening to musicians at the opposite wall play mazurkas, polkas, tarantellas, occasionally a song like "Chitarra Romana," while people danced—and waiting for goodies to pass by was for Tony the essence of a wedding reception. Papa almost never danced. But the spirit grabbed mama a few times during the evening and made her step out onto the spacious, oak-planked floor to dance a mazurka or polka with a woman friend. She was light on her feet, graceful in motion, elegant in comportment.

Not far from the musicians, in one corner, was a table where tap beer was dispensed in glass pitchers. Bride and groom sat at one end of the dance hall, behind a table decked with sandwiches, cream puffs, pastries, and wedding cake. In that order the trays of goodies were passed around the hall, at intervals through the night. The sandwiches were "open," their contents on top of the bread slices, visible through a wax-paper wrapping. Salami, cheese, mortadella (a spiced ham) and capocollo (an aged ham with hot red pepper) were typically included. Beer went well with the assortment, though small children and most women drank soda. Next came the cream puff trays. An ultra-smooth and sweet ricotta with a cinnamon edge to the flavor filled crisp, thin pouches of pastry. These vanished rapidly. At last came the trays of fancy cookies, garnished with tinsel and little sticks of cinnamon coated with colored sugar. The men holding these lavish trays, waiting for people to pick from such exciting variety, had the patience of the saints. Finally, the dance hall cleared, and bride and groom danced solo to "Let Me Call You Sweetheart," while a rotating glittering ball in the ceiling flashed colored specks of light around the hall. This was followed by in-file dancing that made the dance floor undulate with beautiful, winding streams of happy people.

Seafood—mama's love, from having been raised in a fishing city—was for Tony an ordeal, particularly if the creature still tasted "fishy" after cooking. Then there was the slime-and-rubber factor. This ruled out octopus, the calamari beloved of most Italians. And seeing eels swim in the plugged-up kitchen sink prior to becoming dinner turned his stomach. Along with smelly and slimy seafood, Tony threw tripe into the heap of food not to be endured.

The most dramatic food, by far, was capuzzeddri. These were skinned heads of lamb, roasted. There was not much meat on these skulls. Tony would not touch the eyes, and though he liked the marrow in soup bones, he found the similar lamb brains sickening, though others licked their fingers. The tongue, however, suited him, both in flavor and texture.

He did try to taste everything at least once, but often he had to make do with eating bread. If there were cookies, from mama's last baking session, he'd have some with coffee.

In perhaps the smallest kitchen she ever worked in, mama patiently cut the meat off the bones (used for soup), removed the fat and gristle, then cut the beef into ragu pieces or steak-like wraps for *bracioli* or chunks to be ground with the pork for meatballs. Santo and Tony took turns at the grinder. Mama's hands were a marvel to watch, especially when she cut perfect, thin slices of veal for cutlets. By contrast, and not long ago, Tony showed his ineptness by cutting himself drying a knife. He had drawn the blade across the towel with the cutting edge toward his hand.

Mama followed no recipe when she cooked. There were basic ingredients—like olive oil, garlic and tomatoes—and optional ingredients—like seasoning. Always there was room for experimenting. It was fun to try some new ingredient or combination of ingredients, checking the novelty by smell and taste. Always there was a sense of balance in the proportions, instinctively "calculated" to bring about the best results. *Chi ci senti?* Mother would ask son when he came home from school and was given a spoonful or piece of something she had been cooking or baking. "What do you taste in it?" She meant, of course, what new ingredient. She had obviously done something different today. The youngster strained his senses to come up with an answer like bay leaves or anise. Most often the pupil would pass this agreeable test.

Mama went all out. She made pizza. Fancy pastries and cassata decked the tables. The petite Central Avenue apartment buzzed from door to windows with relatives and friends. "This isn't pizza," remarked Sasà Alesi in Sicilian, after Tony's piano teacher sank his teeth into the heavenly dough. "This is sfingiuni," meaning the dough was deep and soft and springy like Sicilian sfingi ("doughnuts").

A part of the school day that Tony especially enjoyed was the walk home for lunch, the check on what had sprouted or started to bloom, what plant needed water, what had come in the mail, and what there was for lunch. Papa's wartime job allowed buying deli staples like tuna in olive oil, capucollu and mortadella (Italian hams), and delicacies like *capunatina*, a canned mixture of eggplant, capons and spices in olive oil and thick tomato sauce, to be eaten sparingly. These items, along with provolone and other cheeses, were *cumpanaggiu*, "with breadage," meaning they were eaten with bread. Eating them without bread invited a scolding. It was not good for stomach or budget to fill up on *cumpanaggiu* alone, without bread.

Some days mama made *frocia* [the zs (not an Italian formation) as in Zsa Zsa Gabor]—an omelet. Typical varieties were fried-potato—with or without onions and peppers—or plain with grated Romano cheese and parsley mixed-in before frying. An occasional asparagus omelet was a special treat. Bread was home-made but sometimes came from the nearby Italian deli.

While the Sicilian mind was hardly a mystery to the lad, Tony would more accurately gauge the temper and style of old-time Sicilians when, many years later, he read Giovanni Verga. He would learn that the duel in *Cavalleria Rusticana* between a man and the one who made love to his wife was not a clean fight, as the opera suggests. The angry husband in fact blinds the adulterer with a fistful of sand before stabbing him to death. While no society has a monopoly on dirty fighting, "La Lupa" ("The She Wolf") comes a bit closer to the extremes embedded in older Sicilian culture. In this story a married field hand warns a village nymphomaniac to keep her distance. But she manages to seduce him while he is resting in the field. He tells her to leave him alone. She persists. In atonement for these sins—the priest won't hear his confession unless "La Lupa" leaves town—the terribly distraught man drags his tongue up the steps of the church. He finally warns that he will kill her if she does not go away. Go ahead, she taunts. He does.

Chapter 5

Sicilian-American Superstitions, Traditions, and Quirks

Mark Hehl

Each culture has its set of quirks and superstitions, some are shared among other cultures and others are unique. Here are some of the Sicilian things that I remember, as a child, growing up in Brooklyn:

-Newborn babies were brought home from the hospital and it was considered bad luck to bring them outside until they were baptized. This was strictly adhered to.

-There were many protective gestures to ward off malocchio (evil eye) such as: placing a yellow bow in a new car.

-There was a need to visit the graves of loved ones as special times such as birthdays.

-My grandmother would always celebrate my Onomastico (Saints Day), which for me was April 25. It was just as important as my birthday.

-If one did not like someone they would spit on the ground when speaking about them.

-We were not allowed to venture outside with wet hair as it was thought to result in one getting sick.

-My grandparents' generation did not trust/believe in Medical Doctors. There was one family health situation that became much worse because of a medical issue which did not receive timely medical attention. An amputation was performed due to the lack of timely medical treatment.

-Wasting food was not tolerated. Children were urged to eat all the food served to them. I believe that this added to my struggle with managing my weight.

-The police were not trusted. Investigations were difficult for them due to the lack of cooperation by the Italians and Italian-Americans in my neighborhood. I know nothing was a common response.

-St. Joseph day was always celebrated in a big way. Other chapters in this book contain additional details.

-Children were to be named after their grandparents. The paternal ones were first. My great-grandmother was named Laura. Being that there were already so many Laura's in the family, my mother was named Lorraine.

-Children were expected to live with their parents until they were married. This was the case with me and my siblings. I attended local universities and spent those years living at my parent's home and not a college dorm.

-When someone was sick or died, the relatives went to church to light a candle.

-I do not remember having ketchup or peanut butter in my early childhood home and to this day I do not eat either. I do not even like the way that they smell.

-It was thought to be a crime if one went to a restaurant for Italian food. That food was always prepared and eaten at home.

Chapter 6

Memory Bits and Pieces

Mark Hehl

As in most Italian-American homes in the 1950s we ate pasta with tomato sauce (*I never heard it called gravy until many years later*) at many, if not most, meals. I remember my mother telling me to stir the sauce every 20 minutes when she went out. We only used a wooden spoon; a stainless steel was not allowed as it was thought to diminish the flavor. When I was young, I incorrectly thought that everyone ate pasta at most meals. As a teenager, I finally realized that only Italian-Americans did so.

In addition to using it to stir the sauce, a wooden spoon was used as a punishing weapon. On many occasions, I was hit with one by my mother for doing something that I should not have done. A wooden spoon brings back memories of the wonderful smell of the sauce simmering on the stove in my childhood home and also the pain.

One day, the sauce was simmering on the stove and a loaf of Brooklyn's famous crusty Italian bread was sitting next to the pot. It was customary to break a small piece off and dip it into the sauce while it was cooking, but only one piece. On this day, my brother and I were talking in the kitchen while dipping the bread in the sauce and got *carried away.* Before we realized it, we consumed all the bread and half of the sauce. We were having some of my parents' friends over for dinner that day and there was not enough sauce left. It took three hours to cook the sauce and there was not enough time to produce another batch. I remember listening to my mother's tirade for the following three days. It was not pleasant.

At about sixteen years old, I was invited to a non-Italian friend's home. They were passing around a bottle of salad dressing and I asked: "what is that stuff?". I have never seen salad dressing before that day. My mother always put olive oil, vinegar, and oregano on the salad prior to serving it. I still do not like prepared salad dressings and eat salad the way that I did as a child. I love olive oil so much that I usually skip the vinegar.

It was not uncommon for a brother and sister to marry another brother and sister in Sicilian-American enclaves. This was the case in my family. My grandmother's brother married my grandfather's sister. This made my cousin, Donna, closer than a second cousin. Donna recounts her memory of celebrating St. Joseph's Day with her grandmother (my great-aunt both by blood and by marriage). March 19 was a special day and still is for Sicilians. On that day, Donna remembers eating pasta with sardines and stuffed artichoke. *Pignolata* (a Sicilian pastry) was placed on a glass plate to heat on the stove. Her mother would give the kids zeppole with powdered sugar in a paper bag to eat on the stoop to avoid the powder from messing up the house. Donna's grandmother had the first color television and she would go there to watch *The Wonderful World of Disney*

Chapter 7

Celebrating a Calitrani Christmas

Joanne Cantarella Ingargiola

Brooklyn, Montclair, Tarrytown, or Dunmore.....close your eyes and you can picture how Christmas holidays were celebrated in every Calitrani household. Officially, the holiday season started on Christmas Eve and Day, continued on to New Year's and concluded with la Festa della Befana on January sixth. The ultimate goal of these festivities during this period was to prepare the perfect holiday table.

I remember as a child, asking my grandparents how Christmas was celebrated in Calitri and what presents they received. "An orange and some walnuts," was the reply with the explanation that these were given out not on Christmas Day but on January 6th by la Befana, an old woman who was looking for the Bambino Gesu. On Christmas Day in Calitri there were the Masses and the singing of songs...no Christmas tree, no decorations, no real presents....but the families did have their traditional meals: fish on December 24th, and chicken on Christmas Day.

Here in Dunmore, we celebrated and celebrated Calitrani style... well, maybe it was Italian style, but in a Calitrani home, we called it a Calitrani dinner. Christmas holidays were always spent at the home of my grandparents, Lucia and Canio Paolantonio. In my family, Christmas Eve started off the festivities. And since it was celebrated according to strict religious custom, it was a day of abstinence. Therefore, no hint of meat appeared on the table. But, in spite of that, Christmas Eve in my household was bigger than Christmas Day. The Italian fish market, Doma's on East Drinker Street, supplied our table with fresh fish to be cooked and served as part of a flavorful and delicious tradition. We would have all different kinds of fish: baccala in sauce, sweet baccalà salad, hot baccala salad, stuffed squids and smelts. There was an orange salad, capellini with olive oil and anchovies, plus the specialty of the house, the stuffed peppers! The recipe originated in Calitri and it is still part of our holiday meal to this day.

Christmas Day was celebrated with another full day's work in the kitchen and typically included antipasto, a homemade macaroni course with a meat sauce flavored with braciole, meatballs and pork. The second course was a roasted turkey served with roasted potatoes, an oil and vinegar salad and vegetables. We'd finish the meal off with roasted chestnuts, fruits and a variety of nuts, pastry, home baked cakes and struffoli, liqueurs and espresso coffee. Naturally, a pitcher or bottle of grandpa's homemade wine was always on the table.

As I mentioned, the holidays were always held at my grandmother's house until she passed away in 1946. Then the dinner preparations fell to her daughters, Aunt Mary Errico and my mom, Antoinette. As our family grew, we had all the holidays at my parents' house on Smith Street. Here, my mother did all the cooking and my sister Lucy, my sister-in-law Helen, and I helped with the usual kitchen and dining room chores. All our families and extended family members were there.

Whether one celebrated Christmas in Calitri or in America, the tastes, smells, sounds, and traditions were kept as close to the heart as possible. Perhaps it was the only time of the year when people put their cares and woes away and celebrated family amid flowing wine and lively music.

Their special dish was stuffed peppers and to this day I still make them. We would buy six Bell peppers or use canned whole sweet peppers in vinegar. The recipe below originated in Calitri.

First, rinse off the peppers. Cut off the stems and remove the seeds. Stand the peppers up in a baking dish. Mix the following ingredients:

2 cups of plain unseasoned bread crumbs
1 tablespoon of olive oil
dash of red vinegar
16 oz. grape jelly.
dash of salt
½ cup of chopped nuts (walnuts or pignoli)
1/2 pound of raisins

The mixture should feel moist. If too dry, add a little more oil and jelly.

Fill the peppers with the mixture. Drizzle the top of each pepper with some oil, bread crumbs and sprinkle lightly with some chopped nuts.

Bake at 350-degrees for 35 to 45 minutes.

Another Calitrani favorite we would make is struffoli. The ingredients called for:

3 eggs
1 1/2 cups of flour
pinch of salt
honey

Combine the eggs, salt, and flour. Mix and knead into a hard ball of dough. Cut off pieces of the dough and roll them out under your fingers to form pencil-size strips. Cut each strip into ¾" pieces. Fry the pieces a few at a time in hot oil until brown. Place each batch on absorbent paper. In a separate frying pan, melt the honey. Turn off the heat and add the struffoli into the warm honey. Stir the struffoli evenly in the honey. Remove the mixture with a large spoon to a plate and shape it into a round wreath. Shake some confetti sprinkles on top (optional).

....

Taken from They Came By ship: The Stories of the Calitrani Immigrants in America, Xlibris Publishers

Chapter 8

Sicilian Christmas Eve at my Grandmother's Home

Erik Hehl

As the first grandchild of Lorraine Hehl, née Rabito, I had the good fortune of spending many Christmas Eves with her and my extended family. The word "spoiled" might come to mind but I believe that I was extremely lucky to have a grandmother who showered not only me but all of her grandchildren with her love. I should add that my Grandma Lorraine shared her home in Queens, New York with my Aunt Valerie, and her husband Louie. Valerie, my godmother, and Louie lived on the main floor and Grandma lived in the apartment on the finished basement level. It was a close-knit household, just as it sounds.

The hugs and kisses (from not only my grandmother but also my aunt) started in the afternoon from the second I came into their door on Christmas Eve and the affection didn't end till late in the evening when it was time to head home for Santa's arrival. I often thought it was a competition between the two ladies, for who could get the most affection in. The Christmas tree (a fresh-cut evergreen, of course) was always decorated beautifully with lots of presents underneath to open later that night. I still remember the nice Rawlings baseball glove she gave me one Christmas, when I was nine, I believe. Treats of nuts and candies including "Hersey's Kisses" were everywhere to indulge upon. Good music (jazz, blues and rock) was DJ'd by my Uncle Louie, which I really enjoyed especially as a teenager. Sometimes the record player even spun Frank Sinatra's "New York, New York", one of my grandmother's favorite.

My memories of that cherished festive time included a lot of homemade food. My grandmother could cook, and she did it well. She was Sicilian and made her own staples fresh, from scratch, including her authentic red sauce (which she worked on all day long), meatballs (as good as I have ever had), pizza (Sicilian-style with a delicious thick crust), antipasti and stromboli with sausage and pepperoni fillings. I also remember her making made a broccoli dish with Italian seasonings and grated cheese on top, as well as large chocolate chip cookies (with added walnuts) that I have yet to find as good elsewhere or duplicate myself. Although we did not have the "feast of the 7 fishes" as many Italians traditionally do on Christmas Eve, we always had shrimp cocktail, which was passed as an appetizer. The evening always culminated with another feast of desserts, with pies, Italian cookies, and pastries as well as coffee for the adults.

Christmas Eve would always include connecting with funny family stories and often a good comedy movie. My father once told a childhood story of throwing life-size dummies off the top of buildings in his Brooklyn neighborhood with his friends that would land below at the feet of unsuspecting pedestrians. I can also remember my father rolling on ground laughing uncontrollably with every funny scene from a movie like Mel Brook's "Blazing Saddles". As the family expanded my role as the family's "squeeze-doll" luckily got passed onto my younger siblings and cousins. The simplest pleasures were often in watching the stumbling infant who was just learning to walk.

Extended family and friends would often filter into the family's home. My Sicilian grandmother was warm and generous with both her family and friends. And Christmas Eve was the culmination of her generosity and love. It was more than just about the food, although that was great part of the Christmas Eve celebration. Maybe we should call our annual gathering the "feast of the 5 senses" as each sense: sight, sound, smell, taste, and touch was satisfied.

I am glad my wife, Jessica, got to spend several Christmas Eves with my family, as well as her mother, Kathy, who visited for at least one Christmas Eve. Too bad our children Jake and Nellie, never had the pleasure of meeting my Grandma Lorraine, who sends her hugs and kisses from heaven for us all.

Chapter 9

An Interview with a First-generation Sicilian-American

Mark Hehl

Giovanni's* parents were born in Eastern Sicily and he grew in the Bushwick section of Brooklyn during the 1970s. Here are his recollections:

Sicilian was spoken at home, so his English was poor when he entered grade school. His teachers recommended that his parents allow him to watch cartoons to improve his English, as ESL programs did not exist at that time.

He lived near his grandparents and remembers the vegetable gardens in the yards of both houses. There was a peach tree that only lasted a few years. The fig tree produced big, long stem fruit year after year. They never purchased vegetables in the summer as thc gardens produced enough zucchini (even the leaves were used for soup), peppers, basil, tomatoes, eggplants, etc. for both households. Tomatoes were canned in mason jars at the end of each growing season.

There were no mega stores at that time. He and his parents shopped at individual stores for each item. There was a store just for cheese where portions were cut with a wire. They went to the pork store for pig products only (no other meat). Toys were bought at a toy store.

The houses were mostly two-family dwellings with relatives living in the other apartment. The doctors had their office in their homes and were available around the clock. Birthday parties were held in basements, most of them were semi or unfinished. The streets were tree-lined back then, and the residents cleaned the sidewalks regularly. The neighbors knew everyone on their block and old ladies leaned on pillows while looking out their front windows during warm weather. The women who worked were mostly employed as seamstresses by the local textile manufactures. Giovanni's grandmother did piecework and often took work home with her. Air conditioners were a luxury that no one could afford, and one was lucky to have a fan during oppressive Brooklyn summers.

Giovanni remembers many of his neighbors sitting on their "stoops" or some of the older folks sitting on their fold out chairs during the late summer evenings trying to catch a breeze.

Giovanni, along with his dad, would travel to Canarsie to buy grapes for the annual home-made wine making.

*Giovanni asked to not be identified

Chapter 10

Growing UP Sicilian in 1950's Brooklyn

Hank Ferraioli

Any memory of a Sicilian upbringing must begin with thought of family. I am sure that my experiences are common ones if you were brought up in Brooklyn in the 1950's. I was literally surrounded by family. Upstairs was my mother's mother, next door and across the street were my grandfather's brothers, around the corner was my father's brother and my mother's aunt and uncle and their children in three separate households. Our front door was never locked. Family and friends alike would rap on the door and walk right in, anytime day or night. A pot of coffee was always on the stove, with pastry and cake awarded to the inevitable visitors. Sundays were busy. Drop-ins were most prevalent after mass when visitors would come by or a short or long visit. The aroma of Sunday "gravy" (tomato sauce, meatballs, sausage, braciole and whatever leftover meat was on hand) would beckon my brother and I to sit down at the table with our parents promptly at 1:00 joined by my mother's sister, husband and son. My Uncle Ray would usually bring Italian pastries from a great bakery on Avenue U. My favorite was the basta chorta, a small, sweet tart with a custard-like center. During those Sunday dinners you would hear Sicilian, Italian, English or a combination of all three. Jokes were usually told in English but the punch lines were always in Sicilian.

The kitchen was the heart of the household. Family and visitors alike would gather around the kitchen table to visit, discuss sports and politics. Almost all my friend's houses had the requisite second kitchen in the basement. Depending on the household, the secondary kitchen would be the primary location for everyday meal preparation or one to be used for holiday meals when extra stove capacity was required. In my house, the basement kitchen was used for holidays and during the summer months. We had a normal sized stove and oven, a refrigerator out of the 1940's (the kind with the circular motor exposed on top of the unit) a double sink and a table.

Holidays were always a special time and my mother would make the usual American holiday entrees, such as: turkey, ham, or lamb. Additionally, they were accompanied by a huge lasagna with all the standard Sunday meat dishes. The meals would seem to last forever, especially after the fruit, nuts and roasted chestnuts would make their way to the table. Similar meals were happening all over the neighborhood.

Christmas Eve was the most special time of the year in Canarsie. My friends' mothers were busy preparing the Feast of the Seven Fishes and my mother was no different. Every household had a slightly different take on which fish dishes were included in the feast. The best part was that the kids would gather is small groups of four of five and "call" on our friend's families to wish them the greetings of the seasons. Family specialties were homemade, and I still have fond memories of the good-natured gatherings. As we became teenagers, we looked forward to a little homemade wine (or sometimes even something stronger). We would all join up together to attend midnight mass and afterwards meet at a friend's home to play cards until the early hours of Christmas morn.

One other major family event in my early years was New Year's Day. It was my paternal grandmother's birthday and all her son's, and their children would gather at my grandparent's home to celebrate. My grandparents had thirteen children, all boys! We would assemble in three different rooms to enjoy a great feast. The rooms were organized by age with my grandparents, their sons and their wives in the dining room, the older cousins at a table in the living room and the younger ones at tables on the closed-in porch. The noise was tumultuous, the food was amazing and the memories indelible.

I grew up in the Canarsie section of Brooklyn a couple of blocks (streets) from Rockaway Parkway. Rockaway Parkway boasted the terminus of the Canarsie Subway (BMT) line, two fantastic pizza places, an avenue lined with small, local shops and Holy Family Catholic Church and School. We also had three different Christian churches and a Synagogue in our immediate neighborhood. Canarsie itself is about a mile square with one edge abutting Jamaica Bay and one boundary formed with Queens. Wikipedia tells us that is was settled by mainly Italian and Jewish immigrants.

We were a large crowd. I remember that on one weekday evening we counted over forty guys and gals "hanging out" on the street corner. We viewed our friends' homes as extensions of our own. A drop-by always entailed an offer of some type of food and depending on the time of day it might even be a full meal. A polite refusal would invariably be countered with "What's the matter you don't like my cooking?" We were always considered "too skinny" or "you have no meat on your bones." I must admit that I had some great dishes during those visits.

I remember helping Pop Petroni in his wine making efforts. He had five sons, the youngest being twins. The twins were two of my best friends and on Saturday mornings in the fall we would haul in cases of grapes, dump them into a huge press and squeeze out the nectar into a large vat. The aromas would make us dizzy and we would laugh and caper around for the rest of the morning. Lunch would be served by Mrs. Petroni who typically offered us fried pastrami sandwiches on Italian bread with pickled veggies and, of course, a small glass of an earlier vintage that was kept in a mayonnaise jar in the refrigerator.

Since most of us grew up with both parents working, after school and Saturday's were totally unsupervised. We were on our own to play ball in the street, or at the park or in the many vacant lots that dotted the neighborhood. For 15 cents we could ride the transit system and go into Manhattan to visit the many museums or other points of interest. Central Park was a favorite since it had the zoo, grass to play ball and lots of paths and interesting sights. Summers would find us hitchhiking to the beaches, Manhattan Beach was our go-to spot, though Brighton and Coney Island beaches were also in reach. As we got older and had access to cars, we often would caravan to Riis Park Beach over on the Rockaway Peninsula. Summer evenings would be dedicated playing softball, volleyball, basketball, and touch football under the lights at the local park.

Brooklyn was an amazing place to grow up in the 1950's and 1960's. We had independence, a myriad of activities to choose from and a community structure that provided safety and support. Oh, and by the way, the food was amazing!

Chapter 11

You Can Take The Boy Out Of Sicily, But.....!

Bill Cimino

My father's family from Messina, Sicily owned a Godfather-esque villa that overlooked the Straits of Messina. My uncle Tony would allow the neighborhood young people to have their wedding ceremony on his property so that once married the couple could walk down the path towards the water. The villa's property was picture perfect and the path was surrounded by citrus trees, oranges (including blood oranges), Meyers lemons, Italian kumquats and limes. Aranci is the Sicilian word for orange and Sicilian rice balls are "arancini" meaning little oranges. Sicily has been a perfect climate and soil for citrus growing and when it was discovered that the cure for scurvy was consuming citrus, the crop became extremely valuable. Since Sicilian government and police was notoriously corrupt, the farmers hired private police to guard their crops. Is it a coincidence that this all occurred when the La Cosa Nostra or "Our Thing" had its origins?

On a separate note, I have my father's old 8mm films, which included a scene with a two-year old me running around my grandfather's back yard with my grandpa who was an avid gardener. Though mine did not scare me with an orange mouth, he had a fake flower which when a bulb was squeezed would result with a fake worm suddenly popping out and back in. I guess Mario Puzo knew all about what he was writing!

Now, my mother's family was from Sciacca, which is a fishing town on the south-west coast of Sicily. My grandfather and his three brothers came to NY and owned several fish markets in Brooklyn, Queens, and Manhattan. He married a woman also from Sciacca, whom he met in NY. That family was also made up of fish mongers. The Bono and Liotta families were well respected in the Fulton Fish Market (except black sheep Uncle Charlie who almost ran it) and when I was in college started working part time with my mother's brother, Joe, who was selling to restaurants after closing his retail store on Nostrand Ave. and Beverly Rd. I eventually went on my own and sold to restaurants (Sheepshead Bay, Staten Island, Flatbush and Bay Ridge) and in the 1980s opened a fish market in Springfield, NJ......the place where Phil Rizzuto would eat my homemade fruitta di mare while filling me with tales of his times as a Yankee shortstop and announcer.

My seafood career came to an end at the end of the 20th century but not before spending years as director of sales for the second largest U.S. producer of live North American lobster, where I assumed the export responsibilities for the company. It was a real pleasure having the opportunity to develop friendships with many importers in Europe and Asia but the principal ingredient of the sweet filling of my seafood cannoli of life became my new friends with seafood businesses in Venice, Naples and Palermo. A proper end to my Sicilian family's rich history!

Chapter 12

Embracing and Living our Beautiful Heritage

Josie Marino

In 1955, we moved into Grandpa Peter's house in Coney Island. I was five years old and adored my paternal grandpa, a gentle widower born and raised in Sciacca, Sicily. Dad's oldest brother and his family lived above us, while dad's other siblings and mom's family resided in nearby Italian neighborhoods in Brooklyn.

We lived surrounded by other Southern Italians, and we treated each other like family. There were grapevines and wine cellars with barrels of homemade wine; fig trees and vegetable gardens; clotheslines with laundry swaying in the salt air breeze; old women who were perpetually dressed in black; men taking naps after lunch; housewives chatting on the stoops in-between their never-ending tasks; older boys playing stickball when they weren't singing doo-wop; we younger kids playing outside all day long until our moms called us home to eat; and doors that were never locked.

Our house was down the block from the now famous Totonno's Pizzeria, the go-place for a pie when unexpected company showed up or for a quick meatless Friday meal. However, this was the exception. Mom and dad were superb cooks, and cooking took center stage at home.

Dad owned a fish store in Bensonhurst. He brought home and prepared to perfection lobster, crabs, shark, mussels, octopus, calamari, snails, porgies, baccala, sardines, clams, and (when they were in season) oysters. His mixed seafood salad was indescribably yummy; while watching him suck the eyes out of the fish floating in his fish soup was indescribably yucky! When working in the kitchen, he would always say that "to live well is to eat well."

Most Sundays we would eat in Grandma Nancy's basement. Grandma and Grandpa Tony hailed from Messina, Sicily, where grandma had been a butcher. Grandma always made her own bread, and for the Sunday meal, her own pasta or ravioli, which she dried on the bed over a clean sheet. As you can guess, Mom's five sisters and their families also came. We kids sat at the special kids' table, where we never needed to be reminded that "children should be seen and not heard."

The rare Sundays we didn't go to Grandma's would find mom at the stove early in the morning getting meatballs, braciole, sausage, pig's skin and pig's feet ready for the pot of "gravy" that would simmer for hours. We hungry kids loved nothing more than breaking off a piece of rustic bread and dipping it in the pot of sauce to stave off our hunger pangs. When we got caught with our hands in the pot, we would get whacked with the moppine.

On Sunday evenings we would sit around the table snacking on dried salami, provolone, cracked Sicilian olives, and lupini beans. Additionally, Dad's superb marinated eggplant and/or his mushrooms and that loaf of rustic bread made this simple meal an extraordinary feast.

This amazing bread came from Mary's Bakery around the corner, which had either a brick or a coal or a wood fired oven. I can still see Mary standing outside in the warm weather with her arms resting on her enormous bosom in between customers and/or baking. Woe be to mom if there was not a loaf of Mary's bread on the table every night. Dad was never to be aggravated when he was eating, and a meal without bread would have been beyond aggravation!

Wine was also present at meals. I remember Dad and his brothers dipping Mary's bread in their glass of wine most times. Summer was the exception, when peaches that had been cut up and left soaking for hours in a pitcher of wine were savored instead.

In addition to family, friends and food, music also played a big part in our lives, which to this day is essential for my heart and soul. Watching the Perry Como show with Grandpa Tony as a small child was a treat, even if I didn't realize then the talent this former barber possessed. Of course, there was always Frank and Dean and Tony and Jerry Vale and Al Martino and Connie Francis and Mario Lanza, and wonderfully wild Louie Prima.

And then somewhere along the way Jimmy Roselli came along. Thanks to open windows in the summer, his incredible voice could be heard throughout the neighborhood. While the Italian words escaped me, I felt something spiritual when this extraordinarily talented man sang Neapolitan classics like "Torno a Surriento" or "Aggio Perduto O'Suonna."

Even dad's brothers, who were tough dock workers, loved Jimmy. It was so comforting when they would all be sitting at Grandpa's table, drinking whiskey, and smoking Lucky Strikes, even though their talking was more like yelling. And when they felt it necessary to start speaking Sicilian, the curses and general gist of their conversation was always understood.

Dad and his brothers named their first son and first daughter after their mother and father. Since there were numerous Peters and Josephines, my cousins and I were all given nicknames, mine being Jo-Jo.

While both my paternal and maternal uncles were special, it was the women and their intangible gifts that stand out.

Grandma Nancy, who was always busy, still found the time to walk blocks to the live chicken market. She would remind me that picking her own chicken to be butchered for dinner was better than the packaged chicken at the supermarket three blocks away. While I loved accompanying grandma, I hated the odor of that market.

When bad odors or anything else caused a headache, grandma did not hesitate to stop what she was doing so she could prepare the oil and water needed to recite the malocchio prayer over us.

This ability to handle the many day-to-day tasks and then anything else that came along with ease and grace (call it sprezzatura or bella figura), to me, is the greatest gift of our heritage. It allows us to be the competent, colorful, determined, passionate, generous, hospitable, warm-hearted, and deeply human people we are.

It also allows me to remember that we are artists of the everyday, taking pride in the details to make everyday life beautiful; and that life's simple pleasures are to be savored and enjoyed to the fullest.

Thankfully, retirement gave me the opportunity to return to our beautiful roots and to live my final chapter, as my father would have said, "like a Sicilian."

Chapter 13

The Pizza Dough Saga

Mark Hehl

My mother always cooked and did it well. There was spaghetti sauce on the stove simmering on many days; yes, just like in the movies. I can still remember the wonderful smell of tomatoes and garlic. Buying the best ingredients was important to her. She would go to various stores or send me for specific fresh foods. Different stores for beef, pork, pizza dough and the live market for chicken. Some stores were far from home. Being the oldest, I was always the one who rode my bicycle to buy these special foods. One hot summer day, I was sent to buy pizza dough. On the way back home, my friends called to me saying: "We need one more for a stickball game, come play." I resisted but they kept tempting me and even held on to my bicycle. It worked, as I did join in hoping to just play for a short time. Losing track of time during this intense street competition, the dough, sitting in the hot sun, expanded, broke the bag, and oozed out between the rungs of the bicycle basket. I did my best to bring the mess into the house. It was falling out over my arms. To say the least, I made another trip to the store and came directly home this time. I did not want to face the consequences from my mother a second time during the same day. I do not remember the details only that my experience was not pleasant. Sicilians tend to be intense and emotional. I grew up on the receiving end of this many times.

Only once I got lazy and bought another item at a closer store and thought that she would not know the difference. It did not work; I got caught. After my mother got finished with her verbal scolding, which lasted a long time, I never even thought about doing it again. Each time after that incident I went to the store that I was told to.

Chapter 14

My Transition to America

Claudio Finizio

First, a short preface to my arrival into the US, which occurred in 1962 when I was twelve. I came from Naples with my family since my father wanted to give his kids (four boys) a better life, which he did. The economic boom in Italy only came about in the beginning of the '70s.

We came through a legal procedure initiated by my aunt, my father's sister, who came to the US in 1925 through what we imagine was a pre-arranged wedding. During that time, an immigrant (her future husband) would write to a marriage broker in the town he came from requesting a bride. When it was arranged (I do not even think that they exchanged pictures) he would take the long trip by boat back to Italy to marry, not to meet and see if it worked, to marry! This still exists in some parts of the world.

Thus, besides my aunt and uncle, I also had three American cousins in Brooklyn, NY. This was the case until some started to move to a far-away place called Long Island.

My early experience was not easy, not knowing the language nor the customs of my new country. It was easier for me at 12 than for my brothers who were older. I also remember the big family gatherings which regularly occurred at my cousin's home in Elmont, NY (a far place from East New York where we lived) due to the fact that my aunt, with my uncle's passing, had moved in with her daughter, my cousin. No matter what the occasion, whether it was a traditional "Italian" feast or a strict American one, mainly Thanksgiving, the menu did not change much. Even though there was a tremendous turkey to cut and devour, the antipasti and pasta were always on the table. The after dinner was even longer with all types of nuts and pastry which were usually mixed in with card games.

Some of the "unusual" experiences I had, also involved food. In Naples one of our favorite dish was "sasiccie e friariell" which in Italian was ''salsicce e broccoli di rape'' fortunately changed to ''English'' sausage and broccoli rabe (big difference that ''b'' made). When I brought to my Catholic High School a sausage and broccoli rabe sandwich (on ''Italian'' bread, of course), some students made fun of it saying that I was eating a weed sandwich. It did not bother me since the taste more than made up for their comments. As I moved on, the same sandwich came back to be an ''important'' part of my life. In college, we started to play cards in the cafeteria, and it was much easier for my American friends to play with one hand while holding their ham and cheese sandwich in the other. I had a tougher time since my sausage and broccoli rabe sandwich needed two hands.

The comments above are some of the happy moments I remember growing up in an Italian-American environment. The neighborhood in East New York (Brooklyn) was full of Italian immigrants so my parents never needed to learn English to either work or shop in our neighborhood. The only time my mother needed to use her English was when she would go shopping on Blake Avenue where the Jewish community put up stands on Sundays. But she managed very well since she knew the numbers ($$$) and no matter what price the merchant would tell her she always answered ''too much''.

Attending high school introduced me to some more non-Italians, mainly Irish-Americans but the big change for me came about when I went to Hunter College in 1967. This institution had just changed a few years back from all girls to mixed students who were mainly of the Jewish faith. What a change from an all-boys Catholic institution!

Chapter 15

My Sicilian Experience

Tony Patti, Esq.

I cried incessantly, or so I was told as we boarded the ship that would take us across the Atlantic Ocean, headed for America. So young, barely four years old, yet so aware of the fact that I was leaving behind my birthplace of Sicily. Along with my sister and my parents, we traversed the ocean and in eight days, it was our turn, a later generation of immigrants from Italy, that would land upon the shores of New York and end up in New Jersey to begin a new life in the New World. Many aunts and uncles, along with so many "paisani" who came both shortly before us and shortly after us, initially settling in tight knit enclaves in New York, mostly in Bensonhurst where, like many immigrants before us, social clubs were set up, restaurants, grocery stores, pastry shops and other reminders of "*u paese*" kept the community connected to the homeland.

I grew up in New Jersey, remembering the many trips across the Verrazano Bridge to visit relatives in Bensonhurst, Brooklyn, being dragged as a kid along with my sister to the Cotillion Terrace banquet hall, for the annual Porto Empedocle Civic Club dinner dance and falling asleep in the car for the late-night trek back to Jersey. My father and uncles opened a pizza shop in Jersey and at 10 years old, I recall going with my father on Sundays to help make the dough early in the morning. My uncle Calogero would give me a Kennedy half dollar for helping and if I folded pizza boxes, he would give me an Eisenhower dollar. I worked at the family pizza shop for many years thereafter, running the kitchen by the time I was 12 years old, learning to make pizza, doing homework in the booths during downtime and learning the work ethic handed down by immigrant parents, aunts and uncles who, like so many before them, sought a better life in America.

I eventually graduated high school, finished college graduating cum laude and when illness befell my father, took out school loans to put myself through law school. The first in my family to earn an advanced degree, I found myself struggling between two worlds and two cultures. Growing up, we spent countless hours together with cousins, aunts, and uncles and unlike the generation of Italian immigrants before us, there was no fear in speaking our native tongue. My siblings and all my cousins spoke our native Sicilian. We enjoyed listening to the stories our parents would tell about the "paese" during holidays and we picked up on the jokes that had us in stitches at times. It was the splendor of being Sicilian, something you just could not understand without knowing the language.

As the years went by and my generation went onto school, moved to different neighborhoods for work or otherwise, it became apparent how difficult it was to retain the cultural connection to our Sicilian identity. It was so hard for several reasons including the fact that Sicilians no longer emigrated to the U.S., upward mobility of the children of the last wave of Sicilian immigrants in the 1950s, 60s and 70s moved out of close-knit neighborhoods in Brooklyn, Philadelphia, Elizabeth (NJ), and moved out to the suburbs, no longer interested in attending social clubs and losing touch with their roots. I missed the large gatherings at holidays, the "barzeletti" (jokes), the food and the neighborhoods filled with so much Sicilian culture. It was disappearing and it was sad. Ironically, it was when I got married with the love of my life, that I was determined to reconnect with my Sicilian culture.

Just as I recall the Sicilian neighborhoods in New York and New Jersey growing up, my wife's family, originally from Abruzzo, grew up in a tight knit community of "paesans" from their town. The difference was, most of them stayed in town, never moving out and practicing their traditions to the present day. I wanted our daughters to experience Sicilian culture. We began taking trips to Sicily when my youngest daughter turned seven years old and my oldest was ten. I brought them to Porto Empedocle, where I was born and by chance was able to stay in the building I was born in, an apartment having been converted to a B & B. The experience was surreal. We returned several times thereafter, each time I was reconnecting with my Sicilian identity and passing on bits and pieces of Sicilian culture to my daughters. My wife was converting herself, falling in love with Sicilian cuisine and the beauty of the island.

As much as the struggles of everyday life in America made it hard to keep the family unit intact, I made it a mission to ensure we ate together as a family and that the food reflected our cultural identity. My children would grow up knowing about Sicily, the history, the island, and the cuisine. I steadfastly refused to let go of my identity and continue to make Pasta con le Sarde every March 19th, celebrating St. Joseph's Day with sfinge from Villabate bakery in Bensonhurst and teaching my daughters that St. Joseph's Day is the real Father's Day and you sprinkle toasted breadcrumbs on your pasta to signify sawdust as Joseph was a carpenter. In December we celebrate St. Lucy's with cuccia, always making my own like my mom did. My kids love it. We have cassata cake on special occasions but always on Easter. We make Sfincione and cudduruni on New Year's Eve and yes, I make my own caponata and as long as I do, my wife will never leave me. A fresh fennel and orange salad cleanse the palate and to help digest, a shot of Averna amaro was a perfect ending to the meal. I still miss growing up with my cousins, listening to stories from parents, aunts, and uncles but I will never let my Sicilian identity die so long as the rich Sicilian blood flows through my veins. Originally from Porto Empedocle (AG), I emigrated to the U.S. young but though I left Sicily, Sicily never left me.

Chapter 16

The Funeral

Richard Rotella, M.D.

A Saturday morning meant no school for me, no work for my parents nor my aunt. My father, a habitual early riser, in his kimono and slippers was shuffling about in the furnished basement. A steady trickling of water from the kitchen faucet could mean he was either shaving, washing out the coffee pot, or filling up the watering can for the houseplants' daily drizzle.

On such a day the others, would usually sleep until well after eight o'clock. Streaming thru the blinds of the window, the rays of the sun teased open my eyes. I tossed about in bed weighing my options.

But this morning was different. The second floor hallway telephone shattered the quiet with its shrill ringing. A bedroom door creaked open and heavy footsteps thumped down the stairs. "Allo Mike?" shouted my grandfather into the receiver. "Hold on Mr. Farina, Mike's comin" came a raspy reply. Then "Allo, allo..deesa Mike?...yeh amma fine tenga-you. Gimme effanowa amma be ready."

Slamming down the receiver, my grandfather bolted up the stairs back to the bedroom. My grandmother mumbled something in her sleep, and rolled over. Within minutes the old man trotted back downstairs, pants half on, suspenders trailing, and arms cradling a shirt, tie, and suit jacket. He began slapping his straight razor back and forth across a leather strap attached to the doorknob of the second floor bathroom. He quickly lathered up and started shaving. Those strange pre-dawn telephone calls were not new to me. They rang every couple of months. From my grandfather's solemn tones, this call could be only from Mike Scalisi, the undertaker, announcing that another lodge member had passed away. My grandfather was president of his lodge, the Acreide Chapter of the Sons of Italy. He was a gifted political 'schmoozer' and had formerly served as an alderman in Lawrence, Massachusetts. On occasion he sold life insurance policies for Prudential. Despite his strong accent, he could navigate thru the intricacies of English as well as any lawyer and therefore became the de facto adviser to a community of laborers and artisans who had emigrated from the eastern shores of Sicily to New York City, many to the Bronx. They were an enterprising, tough and tight-knit bunch. Every birth and baptism, wedding and funeral was attended by the honored Mr. Farina, everyone's 'compare' on demand.

Whenever the call came from Mike, my grandfather would snap to the task with martial readiness, and within minutes would disappear into a formidable black Packard limo waiting for him at curbside to take him to his rendezvous.

This time it was Saturday, and I was determined to root out the mystery of these hurried missions. I bounced out of bed, slipped on my pants and skipped down the stars to where my grandfather was shaving. Peering at me from behind a mask of white foam he blurted "You no gotta school today? You wanna comma widda me? You tella you ma, an betta dressa right away. Mike gonna be eah any minute."

Just as my grandfather had put down his razor and was wiping the last bits of lather from his chin, the telephone rang again. "Allo, who, Oh Mr. Kahn…yeah, yeah I unnah stan…yeah. Mike calla me dissa mo-ning. Ho-kay, I splaina every ting. No worry, I tayka cay-ah. Now I instantly knew who had called. On occasion, I would answer the phone, and Mr. Harry Kahn would be on the line. In his monotone, bass voice he would ask: "You must be Richard ? Would you please tell your grandfather to call me right away. It's important, Thanks." At the click, I caught the after-image of this man. He had a dingy office on the east side of mid-Manhattan, accessible only by the Third Avenue El. My grandfather had taken me there once. In a worn and creaky leather chair sat Harry, partially hidden by a mess of papers and folders scattered aimlessly across a broad desk. A brass lamp with a green glass shade cast a ghostly glow on his long waxy face--a big bear of a man, balding, thin-mustached, square-jawed, wearing a shiny rayon paneled brown vest, the breast pocket stuffed with cigars and a Waterman pen. On the wall behind him hung a regulator clock solemnly ticking away the hours. How could I not recall Harry, moving slowly and deliberately like an elephant, rumbling in his lair under the gloomy shadows of the Third Avenue El.

At that moment It was very clear that one of the 'compares' from the lodge had died. Mike the undertaker, and Harry, the life insurance broker had already known about it, but my grandfather__ was the last to be informed. He began muttering maledictions for not having been told first.

Outside, one mellow honk of a horn announced the arrival of the limo. My grandfather fumbling with his cuff links growled "You gonna comma oh no?" "Yeah, I wanna come", I yelled back as I flew up the stairs to finish dressing. "Tina" shouted my grandfather to my mom who could be heard from the upstairs bathroom gagging while brushing her teeth--"Reech gonna go widda me anna Mike."

"Reech"--screeched back my mother,-- "Comba you hair, an be a gooda boy. Don touch anything, you hear me?" Meanwhile I was glowing with triumph. Wait till I tell Mel and Jerry that I got to ride in a hearse.

Soon the doorbell rang. My grandfather, impeccably dressed, plastered down one of my unruly curls with Brilliantine, and rushed toward the front door. "How a-ya Mr. Farina, memba me, Sal?" came the gravelly greeting. A tall, bulky man in chauffeur's uniform and cap, dark glasses, grinning under a pencil-thin mustache led us down the stairs to a lustrous black Packard funeral director's limo. Mike emerged from the rear seat to meet us. He was broad-shouldered, in his forties, with light brown, wavy hair, clean shaven with cleft chin, wearing sunglasses, and elegantly fitted in a gray striped-pants tuxedo. "whey, Mr. Farina." "whey, Mike," they both yelled in unison, as they exchanged feigned kisses on each cheek. Mike was no stranger to me as I had seen him at previous funerals. But ceremony is a Sicilian thing.

"Deesa my gran-child, Reech" beamed my grandfather. Then nudging me forward and growling --"Say allo to Mike"--"Hello Mike," I peeped, as Mike nearly crushed my fingers with his handshake, and discreetly deposited into my palm a bright shiny silver dollar. "Hello Richy, nice to see ya again, dat's yours, you keep it, whuddaya say you sit inna front seat. Me an yer grandpa, we gotta do some talkin inna back."

'Gee, thanks a lot, Mike" I gasped excitedly. Just as I pocketed the coin, my mother called from the window-"Reech, you forgot your handkerchief." Mike quickly pressed a crisply folded scented hanky into my hand, and muttered "Here, take dis, we gotta get goin Richy."

The limo sped off racing along Pelham Parkway, past the Botanical gardens and the Bronx Zoo, and on to Fordham Road. Then shortly after passing the hospital to our right, we turned sharply left at Roosevelt High School to enter a world within a world. Except for the architecture, here was a detailed reproduction of Southern Italy. The jewel in the crown was the church of Our lady of Mt. Carmel, which already housing a monsignor was ripening up for a bishop. Surrounding this citadel was a sprawl of tenements and shops with a teeming population of Sicilians, Neapolitans, Calabrians and Apulians. This Bronx version of "Little Italy" was commonly known as "Arthur Avenue" a street crammed with shops and markets that catered to every regional whim, taste and fancy. Canopied stands crowded the sidewalks. Shoppers had to maneuver single file past stalls of fresh fruits, vegetables, legumes, fish on beds of ice, live crabs and snails crawling toward the edges of their buckets. Intoxicating smells mingled and clashed amid raspy shouts of shopkeepers coaxing clients to trade at their stalls, all the while jeering their competitors. Inside of a popular bakery stood racks of freshly baked breads in all shapes and sizes, with an extravagant variety of pastries and cookies, and the ever popular cannoli displayed behind glass counters. The latticini store had immaculate walls of white tiles. Stacked like pillars in a temple were wheels of hard and semisoft cheeses, netted balls of provolone dangled from ceiling hooks, freshly molded mozzarella in braids and spheres swam in tubs of brine, freshly drained ricotta exuded a sweet fragrance, and that pungent buttery smell of a dairy wafted far into the street where pizza by the slice was being sold--thin, pliant and oozing with melted cheese, tomato and fresh basil. The grocery stores were a chaos of provocative odors, cans of olive oils, tomatoes, jars of pickled vegetables, tubs of dried beans, nuts, seeds, dried fruits, chilis, figs, dates, oregano, thyme, sage, vats of olives bathing in brine, and dried pastas in every shape imaginable.

The alleys were a din of dialects, Neapolitan, Sicilian and Barese. Mobs of volume shoppers from Queens and Westchester would clog the walkways with their loaded bags, while urchins would run the streets like stray dogs, offering to carry groceries.

Our limo navigated past a stickball game that ended abruptly after the ball had landed on some tall roof. It then swung by the Teatro Gigli and arrived at the funeral parlor. We filed out of the car past a group of smoking bystanders, and went thru the canopied front entrance. The foyer was packed with relatives and friends of the deceased, Turiddu, a plasterer who was born in a town not far from my grandfather's. The parlor was filled with a gentle rumble of voices murmuring in Sicilian. Most of these folks knew one another, but outside of weddings and funerals they rarely met.

Mike, my grandfather and I weaved our way thru the crowd, here and there exchanging greetings, finally entering the viewing room. The open casket was engulfed in floral wreaths and bouquets of roses, carnations, gardenias, whose combined fragrance was intoxicating. About the room were statues of the Virgin Mary, St. Anthony, and a large painting of the Resurrection, each with a small kneeling platform before a stand of votive candles. I lit a candle and delighted in watching the dancing flame until my grandfather nudged me out of my reverie and on toward the front row of folding chairs that were reserved for the immediate family of the deceased. He gently gathered both hands of a plump and pretty, rosy-cheeked black-clad woman, probably in her forties, and kissed them. They traded whispers, as he mopped a tear rolling down her cheek with his handkerchief. I soon recognized her under her black veil to be Turiddu's widow Nanuzza.

A recurring theme of conversation at our table was the tragic marriage of Turiddu and Nanuzza. My grandfather was among the first to know of the latest atrocity committed by this man against his wife. Gradually I was constructing an image of life under this bully and his helpless victim. On those days when Turiddu was out of town, Nanuzza would drop by the house to spill her heart out to my grandmother, while helping her shell fresh fava beans out in our back yard. Glancing at the occupant of the casket and then back to Nanuzza's tearful face, It dawned on me that the final respite usually comes with the death of such a brute. With the few years she would have left, she could at last have the time and solitude to discover her inner self. The face of the widow clearly revealed that her life with Turiddu was sheer martyrdom.

The Great War had recently ended and the Bronx was in the midst of a construction boom. Skilled artisans like Turiddu were in continual demand. On the job site, he was always the first to appear and the last to leave. Compulsively perfectionistic, unfailingly on time and painfully frugal, Turiddu was never without work. In just a few years he owned his own modest house, a car and was saving enough to eventually become an independent contractor. The deceased was good natured and generally admired. But like a vicious dog, he could sense whenever someone was afraid of him, and this would encourage him to attack at whim. He would goad, and bait anyone who showed timidity. He would entertain his comrades with tedious jokes, that he topped off with an ear-splitting hyenalike laugh. His favorite victim was Santo the village idiot. Just as every village in Sicily has its patron Saint, it sadly also has its designated idiot. If a family of means had a retarded child, before any outsider could become aware of this, the child would have long been spirited off to the care of some relative from a distant village, or to a religious cloister. But Santo was born to a wretchedly poor family, which was stuck with him. One could describe the boy as moderately retarded, illiterate, yet gifted with gab. He had an unexpectedly rich vocabulary, and an agile facility with mockery and satire. Idiot that he was, he often forecasted bad happenings such as an illness, accident, or even an untimely death that would befall a fellow villager. For this rare gift of clairvoyance he was held in considerable awe, and was not infrequently asked to deliver a prophesy. Yet Santo spent much of his wakeful day as a child trapped in an adult body, amusing the townsfolk with his capers and antics, running after butterflies and frolicking with the goats.

This village idiot invariably caught the attention of then adolescent Turiddu, who for several ensuing years became his chief abuser and tormentor, showering him with interminable taunts, insults and threats, until came Santo's day of deliverance the day that Turiddu had packed his suitcase, and was off to a new life in America. Whatever became of his favorite victim Santo is greatly conjectural. His name rarely would come up at the dinner table, but rumor has it that he found work on a merchant ship, and had seen a lot of the world.

Many years had gone by. In his new American role, Turiddu had accommodated easily and well. But his basic nature of hale and hearty bully was immutable. He loved to relate to his circle of friends the many times and ways he had humiliated and compromised Santo, the idiot. Turiddu had the particularly bad habit of speaking with a mouth full of food, with all its attendant spitting and drooling. One evening while hosting a dinner for a group of admiring cronies, just as he was reaching the punch-line of one of his jokes, he began gasping for air, quickly turned blue and stopped breathing altogether. An ambulance rushed him to nearby Fordham Hospital where he was pronounced dead from asphyxiation and a ruptured esophagus...the result of having choked on a piece of boiled beef.

Lying there in state was Turiddu, once the healthiest of men, with a smooth florid complexion, curved sensuous lips smiling sardonically. The guests hushed "why he looks so real," while another quipped "Yeah, they sure did a good job."

While Mike was fumbling with papers in the office, the mourners began lining up before the casket to pay their last respects, cross themselves, touch the dead man's forehead with two fingers, then to their lips, and the ritual farewell was over. Mike reappeared, approached the casket, paid the body a brief homage and addressed the assembly. "Cari amici, the priest is here to say the prayers before we close the casket and go on to the church for the service. Anybody that wants to say a last good-bye to Mr. Messina should do so now."

At the entrance of the viewing parlor, the priest paused for a few moments before nimbly weaving his way thru the throng toward the closed casket. He was in his thirties, with ample wavy black hair, thick arching eyebrows, and a long, aquiline nose. He was acutely aware of his sensuality. As his shining black eyes autonomously scanned the crowd for adolescent girls, his lips curled in delight from watching them blush, giggle and squirm under his provocative gaze. Then signaled by a sense of mission he turned to his breviary, searching for the section on 'prayers for the dead.' He was about to begin when....

All of a sudden a commotion arose from the rear of the room. A disheveled creature, moaning, chuckling and gesticulating, pushed his way thru the crowd toward the casket. People retreated from his path. The priest backed away, recognizing something unwholesome in this intruder. In a rumpled suit, a wild mane reaching his collar, the stranger stood for a moment before the casket. Then with uncanny strength, lifted the lid and leered madly at Turiddu's corpse.

"Finalmenti, iu sugnu ccaffora, e tu sì daddindra." he cried out. "Però oggi comu pari beddu ripusatu, tuttu profumatu e pittinatu, Cu ti fici a barba sta matina? Unni vai? Nnô paradisu? Oh no, tu stai iennu a lu nfernu unni apparteni, figghiu di bona matri."

The man then grabbed the deceased by the torso and tried to extract him from his casket, but a group of men pounced on him, restraining him, as he bellowed and cackled maniacally. Someone had called the police, and within minutes a patrol car screeched to a halt outside. The mourners stood in stunned silence, as Mike and his assistants dragged the man, kicking, and screaming out of the funeral home into the arms of the police.

Before disappearing into the police car, the disruptor was heard bellowing… "Nun ti scurdari, a mía mi chiamanu Santu, e cu tocca a mia, nu santu tocca." The mourners were paralyzed with shock and confusion, as Mike tried to reassure everyone that the service would continue without any further transgressions. The sobbing widow was surrounded by friends who embraced and kissed her, whispering gentle reassurances. As the commotion died down, the priest decided to take control, and standing before the casket began reciting the Rosary. After this round of prayers was over, Mike again addressed the crowd, giving instructions on how to reach the church and thence to the burial grounds.

Four pallbearers stood by either side of the casket, and at an imperceptible signal lifted in unison the heavy load onto their shoulders. They paused, shifted their feet, braced their shoulders, got their balance and shuffled off toward the awaiting black hearse.

My grandfather said his final goodbyes to the immediate relatives as they filed into their reserved limo. He would neither attend the church service, nor the burial. The lodge was going to pay all the funeral expenses, and it was up to him to negotiate a fair cost with Mike.

My grandfather and I took the bus home, but I recall what I had heard him whisper into Mike's ear before leaving: "Era Santu, lu scimunitu dû paisi".

Chapter 17

San Giuseppe...Sicilians Love You

Constance Miceli, DSW / Ph.D.

Who can explain why St. Patrick is so revered by Irish Americans and St. Joseph, the father of Jesus, and the husband of our Blessed Mother is hardly remembered on March 19th, except for older, devoted Sicilians who still regard him as their patron saint? For me and my family that is sad and disappointing.

My life, raising five children, working, and attending graduate classes at Fordham University was way too busy to think about researching the importance of St. Joseph to my husband's parents, who emigrated from Sicily. We listened to their interesting stories of "la tavola" and the feeding of poor families, but never knew that so many other Sicilians revered him or why.

We did know that my husband, our five children and I, were expected at grandma and grandpa's house on March 19th, for the special foods that were prepared. Only severe illness was accepted as an excuse not to arrive before dinner.

Hence, for countless years we trekked from our home in East Norwich, after work and school, to the Micelis' home in Middle Village, Queens to celebrate and honor St Joseph. The ritual and meal were always the same! The framed, huge painting of St. Joseph was removed from storage and hung on the kitchen wall where we could pray to him before we ate. The prepared meal was one that neither my children nor husband liked, but they were polite and somehow managed to swallow.

The main course was "pasta con sarda' cooked with fresh sardines and fresh fennel in red sauce served over "bucatini" pasta....(like spaghetti but with a hole thru it), and "fritto misto"...(batter-dipped fried fresh vegetables), green Sicilian olive salad and a greens salad. My children referred to this meal, as "pasta with grass and gravel' because fennel looked like grass and, breadcrumbs toasted in a pan with olive oil and garlic was sprinkled on top of the pasta instead of parmesan cheese. This looked like gravel to the children.

Of course, we all saved room for dessert, the famous zeppoli made at the pasticceria, was an especially scrumptious treat for us with espresso and Sambuca. To this day, I do not know how my in-laws did all that cooking in their tiny kitchen, served us graciously with a smile, at a table, in the living room, and cleaned up afterwards. We departed early with the children, on school nights, and did not help. In retrospect, I am deeply grateful to my in-laws for this wonderful family tradition. Their faith in St. Joseph was lifetime and sincere, and their hospitality to local poor families was generous.

After they passed, my second oldest daughter decided to carry on the tradition as best as she could. She wanted her two children and my husband, whose name is Joseph, to continue honoring our patron saint, who was always responsive to our prayers.

As we got older and had time to reflect, my husband and I recalled we were both christened at St. Joseph's Church in Brooklyn. As children, we received our first holy Communion and Confirmation there. We attended many street festivals, as teenagers, to enjoy "sazizza" heroes, and "sfinghi" cooked in boiling hot oil sprinkled with powdered sugar. These good memories and nostalgia led us, when we were in our 80s, to re- visit the St. Joseph's Church we loved. It was still the same as we remembered it.

There is one more coincidence: when we bought a condo in Florida, we learned that the parish church for our community was named St. Joseph. Upon arriving there, we were greeted by a life-sized statue of St. Joseph.

In the final hours of my husband's life, I did not know that the hospice was across the road from St. Joseph's Church and statue. This was a nice surprise to learn that St. Joseph was watching over my husband after he passed. <u>Note</u>: my husband's father was born in San Giuseppe Jato, Sicily.

It would not be an exaggeration to say that St. Joseph has been in our family's life from birth to death. For his blessings, guidance, and ever - presence, we are eternally grateful!

Chapter 18

Sicilian Family Memories from Louisiana

Joseph L. Cacibauda

The sagas of American/Sicilian immigrants generally tend to locate their stories within urban America, notably in the Northeast and Midwest. Ports of Ellis Island, Portland, Maine, Boston to name a few were immigrant gateways and many of those people remained in these areas, or fanned out westward toward Detroit, Chicago, St. Louis to work in mines, railroads, and factories, or open their own shops. Other immigrants disembarked at ports in Pascagoula, Mobile, Galveston, Pensacola, Miami, and New Orleans, the southern ports, and they stayed and worked in these areas. The Italians that went to California and Colorado, further west, usually came through the Port of New Orleans. There was an early period of immigration to the south when Sicilians were actively recruited by sugar and cotton plantation owners to supplement the dwindling black labor force recently dissipated through the Emancipation Proclamation. My book *After Laughing Comes Crying* chronicles this history in Louisiana. Due to the ravages of the civil war, lost crops, the costs of rebuilding, the falling prices of sugar, the increasing costs of labor, and other reasons, plantation owners began liquidating their lands and holdings. Their Sicilian workers, living Spartan lives, hoarding their monies, were prepared to buy sections of the lands. These new landowners created a class known as Italian truck farmers, tilling small acreages, and selling produce at local markets. My grandfather was one of them. As a child I accompanied my father (as he accompanied his father) to the French Market, along the river in New Orleans where he would back his car to a stall and sell garlic from the trunk—elephant garlic, a dozen heads skillfully plaited to the string, $1.50 a string. The French Market truck farmers sold all varieties of produce and it was a sight to see and hear them as their constant banter bounced off the market's roof, echoing Cajun French, Spanish, Sicilian, Italian, blended with English. There were friends and relatives that met there from different homesteads, sitting on over-turned bushels, wooden crates, or buckets, cleaning and rearranging watermelons, potatoes, tomatoes, corn, their produce, while waiting for customers to come by. In the urban sections of America, Italian émigrés, farmers in the old country, were unwilling to abandon their agricultural knowledge and acumen as they were compelled to work in factories and elsewhere; so, they found ways to grow things in the cities. A friend told me of his Italian father in Chicago who had a fig tree and each winter he would fold the tree in a particular way and cover it with layers of newspapers to protect it from the harsh Midwestern winters, and then nurse it back to health in the spring. My college roommate introduced me to his grandfather in New Jersey who lived in a row of city houses but was able to dedicate a small plot of land next to his house to grow tomatoes, beans, corn, and garlic. Even in New York city, tenement dwellers had roof gardens. I believe they still do. For these "old-time/old country Italians", no matter where they landed in their new worlds, they maintained a key trait common to most of them: the need to always busy their hands to yield something useful. To this end, they planted trees for fruit, garden plants for vegetables, and raised animals for food. If the tree gave shade, the vegetables flowered, the animals became domesticated, they were so much the better for the beneficent byproducts. Their old country subsistence dictated they constantly produce something from their lands and with their hands. In Mary Taylor Simeti's book, *On Persephone's Island*, she tells of hiring a Sicilian driver to get her across the island and on the way, the car has a flat tire. The driver was able to get someone (before cellphones you understand) to bring help and while they waited on the side of the road, her driver sauntered off into a field of tall grass and cleared it.

In my Sicilian family, I was ever aware that my father and mother rarely moved from point A to point B without creating something while on the way. If they sat on the porch swing, they snapped beans, or shelled pecans, or peeled or cleaned something. My brother spent years filling a five-gallon water jug with spare change. While visiting him, my parents noticed the full jar and when my brother returned from work, they had emptied the jug and counted the change. If my dad walked outside, he had a mission, and usually did not return without having finished it. He might be outside until after dark. This was after a full eight hours work shift. Neither parent ever complained about work. Never. And this was true for my aunts and uncles. They had no "hobbies." Their leisure times involved making something—cooking, sewing, mending, crocheting, building, creating furniture; or fixing something—a car, a tractor, a machine, a roof, plumbing, electrical and on and on. To get my dad to visit me out west, I would be sure to have a project for him to make it worth his while to travel there. His greeting to my wife on the phone was never, "How are you? or How's everything?" it was, "Where's Joe, working?" With this penchant for productive work, our earlier family visits and get-togethers often were paired with pending projects. A weekend or a Sunday visit might include the visitors helping the hosts dig a well, or plant/harvest a crop, or frame a house, or drywall a room, or dress a butchered animal, or prepare foods and *dolci* for some special occasion, perhaps a religious celebration.

My fondest memories of family get-togethers are those spent at an aunt's house in small *comune* around Baton Rouge, Louisiana. We lived in southern Louisiana around New Orleans. The *comune*, called Fordoche, was located north-west of Baton Rouge; and was my father's birthplace. Our family referred to it as "up the country," and we occasionally would go "up the country" to spend weekends with my aunt and her family. There were no super highways, or freeways, in the 50s, only two lane blacktop roads that ran from New Orleans to Baton Rouge, snaking through cane fields, farms, rice fields, dairies, wetlands, and occasionally going by a refinery or sugar mill. Turning off the highway, we headed west onto a graveled road toward Fordoche, we seven, packed into a 40's Oldsmobile sedan, carrying popcorn, home-made cookies, Kool-aid, and who-knew-what-else for snacks. There would be no restaurant stop for lunch on the 112-mile trip.

Arriving at the remnant of a fence, sagging, tangled barbed wires enmeshed in blackberry and wild bushes, posts leaning, broken if not altogether missing, we turned into an opening onto a long clam shell drive, shelled only in the tire tracks, and we'd drive up to a small white house, commonly known in the south as a Cajun cottage. The front porch of four posts supported the somewhat rusted galvanized roof that stretched from the house peek and dropped down, like a large chute, to cover the porch. Up two or three steps, hovering over the porch's deck, held up by chains, were two latticed bench swings facing each other from opposite sides that perpetually seemed to sway. Looking to the left of the house, one saw a huge oak tree under which my dad would park the car, and where its umbrella constantly shaded a space for outdoor sitting. My uncle was usually waiting there, in a chair, leaning forward over crossed legs, elbow on a thigh, Camel cigarette in one hand and a cup of chicory coffee, black, in the other. In due time, my aunt would come out, all smiles, arms wide opened, to greet us, in Sicilian, "Eh chi un' bedda famigghia. Ahh Senuori biatu." Then we would all line up to kiss her and our cousins in the Sicilian way, on the mouth (a greeting I thought every Italian did until I was well into adulthood. One friend would tell me: "I hated to go with my friend Sony Cusumano because I had to kiss all of his relatives on the mouth.")

My aunt and uncle's house built perhaps in the 20's, maybe earlier, had four rooms. There were two bedrooms, one in the front and one in the back. From the doorway, a large living room was set to the right and a bedroom was to the left. There was a fireplace in the living room. A small kitchen was in the back and stood to the right of the back bedroom. There was no bathroom in the house but rather an outhouse that stood away from the rear and an enclosed shed that housed a galvanized wash tub that the grown-ups filled with bath water when the need arose. For this visit, my aunt and uncle were prepared to sleep and feed our seven, plus their own seven.

Of an evening, when the news of our arrival got out, people would come by—an uncle, sometimes a few of my father's childhood friends. The men sat on the porch swings or on the deck in conversation well past midnight, their Sicilian/English words muffled in the dewy air as they chatted through clouds of pipe, cigar, cigarette smoke. We children played on the damp front lawn, sometimes catching fireflies in jars, or smashing them against our shirts to gross out the girls and to show the remnants of their glow; or we just played hiding games in the dark. As hours passed, the porch conversations waned, and visitors gradually left. Our mother and aunt would prepare the living room for all the children. As many could fit, we slept on the floor with the smaller children sleeping in the adults' bedrooms.

In the morning, early, the heat of the cooking stove warmed

our sleeping room and carried the smells of chicory coffee, bacon, eggs, baked bread, and the sugary whiff of sweet rolls in the oven. Permeating the warmth and scents were the sounds of low murmurs and faint movements, my aunt and my mother chattering, pinging metal and scraping wooden utensils to some purposes; cups, forks, knives, plates slightly clanged as the women placed them on the metal table. The men were already outside under the tree drinking coffee, smoking cigarettes, engaged in their own conversations. Still a bit drowsy, I recall laying there comfortable and cozy in the appreciation of these simple, make-do accommodations, this secure and loving setting. These were the days of familial well-being and joy.

In keeping with productive purposes, I recall one visit to Fordoche when we helped cut and bale hay in readiness for the winter. The area's larger and more industrious farmers rented their machinery to the smaller farmers for the job. We children ran behind the loud, rattling baler as it gathered, tied, and then dropped off the hay. We loaded bales onto a tractor's trailer that hauled them to the storage barn. The work was strenuous, the day was hot, and the reward was fresh slices of watermelon served and eaten under the oak tree. We all knew that my uncle could have, would have, cut and baled his field without our help as indeed he did every year; but, as I look back at that particular visit and those others alike, our child's pride came from being able to help, and being a part of accomplishing something that needed to be done. Perhaps such chores helped awaken and fortify our engrained Sicilian notion of work.

Of course, as we were out in the field, the women prepared the next meal. There was a pork roast cooking in the large pot of *sugu*. The tomato sauce began simmering as soon as all the ingredients were added, just after the breakfast chores were completed. As the women "relaxed" they prepared all the elements for dinner, cutting vegetables, boiling eggs (there were always a few hard-boiled eggs floating in the red sauce). The pasta was macaroni, *maccheroni* in Sicilian. To us, there was no other pasta but macaroni, the long fat tube pasta. Of-course we had other pasta, but our generic name for pasta itself was macaroni. I remember my father visiting me out west and I took him to a fancy Italian restaurant. In my youth I had not yet realized that to Italians, no one's cooking meets their home-cooked standards. Nevertheless, I suggested my father order the Pasta Alfredo (which by the way is hardly ever found in Italy, maybe in an American run Italian restaurant). He ordered and when it came to the table, he asked how much I had paid for it. I lied. I did not want to tell him the real price. His response was, "Hell, this ain't nothing but macaroni and cheese. I could'ah made this for a couple of dollars."

The meal finished the men sometimes helped by bringing in water pumped from the well just outside the back door to wash dishes. The scraps were put in a bucket to be fed to the chickens and the pigs. The old dish water was thrown over the side of the small back porch scattering the chickens, dogs, cats, whatever animals that might have been settled there. The night's talk session would begin anew on the front porch swings, this time with the wives included. Meanwhile we played board or card games in the living room until our moms prepared the sleeping area again. The next morning, early, we would pack up the car and drive back to New Orleans.

Sadly, there is little, or nothing left of our grandparents' and parents' ways and customs. We third and fourth generation Sicilians were privileged to have experienced many of them first-hand: their foods, *feste*, smells, utensils, words, proverbs, stories, admonitions, curses, gestures, their Sicilian language. We are the last generation to recall old country wise and unwise uncles, aunts, *compare, comare*, priests, nuns, *nonni*. But, like most of our parents, we too failed to keep what we knew alive in the course of earning livings and surviving this American life. In some cases, our lack of defining our Italianism has allowed Hollywood to frame us in inaccurate and distorted pictures that produce shame for those who do not know better. But our world is not the world of our parents and our childhoods. In today's world our family lives are at the mercy of technologies where their everchanging pace determines how, how much, what we do and where we go to work. Our families are no longer confined to small neighborhoods or local settings of like nationalities with unspoken but understood norms. Our children have ventured out into the world of diversities and have often chosen to stay in those environments, choosing mates from other national cultures and values. Old ways are lost in the unions and new family trends emerge.

I am hopeful that there will be those who will be curious enough of their Sicilian heritage to want to learn it, keeping it from evaporating into history. But then, it is not enough to read and learn customs without practicing them. Consider that we Italians visit Italy and take cooking classes to learn the old Italian ways; but then we opt to leave those learned lessons in Italy. It is enchanting to make *lu pani* from scratch at a Sicilian *agriturismo*, but time consuming and seemingly unrealistic to spend a full morning making it at home. While paying to learn pasta making at an Italian villa, back home, we often complain about the time it takes the water to boil and a box of pasta to cook when we need to be somewhere else. Many of us remember old country recipes and ways, but do not take the time to bring them into our lives or share them with our own.

To my mind, our Sicilian ancestors are heroic historical figures, because of their American contributions and legacies. It is appropriate that we 3rd and 4th generation American/Sicilians use romantic colors to paint pictures of the old country and put our ancestors in embellished frames. Hopefully, coming generations will view them and in the same spirit we portray, keeping the dust off the pictures we have created by learning the culture, history, and ways. Thankfully, Arba Sicula has preserved histories and the language and customs of the old country in books, CD's, journals, articles, and programs. There are organizations that are promoting online Sicilian/English translations and dictionaries. There are social media groups that share things Italian and Sicilian. These developments are encouraging. For those of us who still remember the "old-time/old country Italians" we can share those things through our writing and support each other in our remembrances. Having done all we can, we can only hope for the best.

Joseph L. Cacibauda is the author of the books: *After Laughing Comes Crying* and *Not For Self: A Sicilian Life and Death in Marion*

Chapter 19

Family is Everything for Sicilians

Devon Hehl

My Sicilian grandma was not your average grandma. A quiet, gentle, docile, and aged individual, she was not. With a wardrobe of wild glasses and sunglasses, a fabulous collection of dangly earrings, and clothes so vivid you would feel outdated next to her, she easily filled any room with life and energy. Yes, my grandma had style and zest - that, anyone could see and feel just being around her a little while. And if you had the pleasure of being close to her by blood or not, you would understand the meaning of "La famigghia è tuttu".

My grandma took care of us all, especially in the kitchen. We would always end up near or in the kitchen every visit to grandmas. Upon entering the house, you would smell her sauce bubbling away on the stove. Taste buds would start watering anticipating the meatballs and sausage that would accompany that sauce and spaghetti, cavatelli, or penne. Once you made it to the table, a frenzy of spoons and forks and chatter filled the kitchen. If you did not ask for seconds, you were crazy (unless you were a kid who was saving room a homemade delicious cannolo)! This was what it was all about: family sharing life and food together.

Grandma spoiled us all rotten, which is why we all waited anxiously until the next sleepover at our Aunt Valerie's house. You see, my cousins lived in a two-family house in Queens Village, NY with my grandparents. Part of me always felt a teeny bit jealous knowing they got to spend so much time with our grandparents. Our time away, however, made each weekend there so special and fun. Grandma took us shopping, to the movies, and out everywhere. She had a friend living down the street with an incredible inground pool - this was always a highlight, as we grew up without a pool or access to one. Her friend also had an enormous fridge full of goodies each time we went. We were not only spoiled with the typical overindulgence of sweets, staying up late, and watching movies beyond the G-rating, but those weekends overflowed our cups with love and lots of laughter.

Grandma Lorraine was not afraid to say what was on her mind or even let out a swear or two in Sicilian, even in front of us kids. That kind of free-flow, family banter was what kept our visits alive and full of giggles that left your face flushed. Everyone had their turn as the 'butt of the joke', though usually my dad and grandpa got most of it thrown their way. This was part of what it meant to be family, with my grandma at the heart and very center of it all.

It is clear to see that the phrase "family is everything" has the heart as its center. And this often has me thinking of times that warm my heart. One of those times for me and my family used to be Christmas Eve. Our day usually began by getting up and ready to head on into New York City. More than one car left the house as years went by and our family grew to include partners and even grandchildren. First stop was not Grandma's though. Instead, it was somewhere that became such a simple, yet pleasurable part of our yearly journey. Deep in the Belmont section of the Bronx, you will find a street (Arthur Ave.) that houses some of the best Italian delicacies in New York. This is where we would go from shop to shop waiting in line as others gathered up their cannoli, Italian cookies, fresh bread, and mozzarella balls to take to their families for the holiday.

Finally, we would make it to Queens, where my aunt and uncle lived with my grandparents. We knew which house it was, as it was always outfitted with blow-up Santas or snowmen and lights around the windows. As we walked up the steps, we were usually greeted by my Uncle Louis, one of the warmest and gentlest souls I have ever met. I could hear Christmas music playing in the background, the jazzy kind, and see the tree in the corner all lit up. Grandma was usually sitting on the L-shaped couch snuggling with someone who had just arrived. Grandma's snuggles were fierce and even included a pinch on the bum. In fact, I will never forget the made-up song she used to sing to us as kids "I got the little culo, and it's oh so cute."

The night continued with everything revolving around the meal, as this became one of the ingredients, like glue, that held us together. Pasta with sauce, fish, sausage and peppers, mozzarella, olives, fresh bread, and broccoli rabe were always on the menu, followed by the delicious pastries and cookies brought in fresh from The Bronx. We ate, laughed, told stories, and enjoyed each other's company, creating memories to last a lifetime. These memories, like parts to a recipe, stay in my mind and heart every year as I remember my Sicilian Grandma and the times I had.

Chapter 20

My Italian / Sicilian Soul

Louisa Calio

When one refers to soul there are many possible associations that come to mind: religious, cultural as well as musical. The way Thomas Moore defines soul in his philosophical book, Care of the Soul, is as a deeper Self connected to family, ancestry, all profound attachments, and life's particulars, as well as shadow or repressed sides of us.

I like to think of my American self, the persona born and raised in Brooklyn, New York, as a metaphor for my spirit, while the part of me that lived at home was my soul. Growing up in Brooklyn, in the 1950s in my grandparents' Italian home was quite a mix. While my intimate world had many Italian customs, beliefs, and traditions, I also had Howdy Doody, Davy Crockett, Mickey Mouse and all the dreams of post-World War II American children. To boot, I was born on the 4th of July, which many in my family considered a good omen. I lived near the Statue of Liberty and loved the American hero, Superman. I sang songs my father brought home like, "Old Soldiers Never Die" and "Jimmy Crack Corn". I owned the first Howdy Doody Puppet in my neighborhood and felt part of an old frontier I had never seen with a Davy Crockett coonskin cap, as well as battles for and against an England I did not know. Not until I was in college in the late 1960s and grad school in early 1970s, did I feel the need to explore and actualize a part of my being that had little connection with this frontier tale. It identified with darker others, their struggles, rituals, with the ways of people like Native Americans and African Americans, as well as journeys to the African continent.

I found my Sicilian roots by way of Africa, a continent I never planned to visit, but ended up making several trips to. Africa came into my life from early childhood. I fantasized myself as an Egyptian priestess dancing to middle eastern music and dreamed of Bedouins in long billowing robes, riding across the dunes on Arabian horses, sometimes with me on the back. One Halloween at the age of 16, to relieve some of the hold the fantasy had on me, I dressed in purdah from toe to head, covering myself completely in a pale blue robe and veil. I could barely see or speak. Yet, I confess I felt a power in invisibility, a truly secret observer, a spy in the world. I understood that to be covered is to be the void, a hidden potential ready to be fulfilled by your lover or husband or parent's request or any external projection. Islam veiled women and the Moors had conquered Sicily. Perhaps this had in part accounted for my dreams and a need to explore this territory within me and those lands.

There was also my Catholic upbringing, where the figure of the Madonna in blue veil dominated. She was the mysterious woman, virgin and mother who stood for compassion and tenderness. Later she would be revealed to me as the Great Goddess Isis from Egypt, the same Goddess brought to Sicily as the Black Madonna. As a veiled woman, one gets to be the mirror and know oneself through the other, but at this same party, when the music was turned up, I found I wanted my freedom to move and dance. I pulled off my robe and veil and danced my heart out to the rhythms of soul music.

Thomas Moore, like Jung, suggests the more one effort to leave something, to be other, the more likely we are to repress those qualities that later come back with a bite! America had a way of doing that for immigrants, promising wonderful new opportunities, a chance to leave the past behind, to escape generations of limiting beliefs based on class, history, inertia. My grandfather often said America was full of bright ideas that were not well thought out, like the automobile, which might come back to haunt us. He never understood why we did not develop the rails like Europe did.

My Sicilian roots haunted me in other surprising ways. By age 20, I met and started seeing an Eritrean, who spoke Italian, while I could not. He came from a culture where women were expected to play traditional roles. My soul seemed to come from many places and many of them had both a rich ancient history and a history of female subjugation. I noticed that this side of me was introverted, bookish and had a deeper darker aspect that called me to ancient Greek and Egyptian myth, with a steady somber song playing in my heart.

My family on my father's side was 100% Sicilian. I associated

Sicilians with an amazing focus and adaptability. My father's mother, Luigia Gianno was born in Palermo. Her husband, my grandfather, Antonino Calio was from Agrigento.

They had a great love that broke family ties and rules, eventually taking them to America where Nino died at age 50 when my father was a boy of 12. When my grandparents arrived in America they had to start over at new careers. Although my father's mother was educated in music, she learned pattern making and became a designer in New York City, working all her life in the garment industry. My grandfather, a businessman selling surgical instruments, became a presser and died suddenly from pneumonia. Most of grandmother's family still lived abroad, some in Palermo, Rome, and a few in Libya, until driven out by war. We rarely heard about them or planned to visit.

We had a cousin from Palermo come to live with us to attend medical school in America, but he never spoke about our Sicilian roots either and quickly married an Irish girl. My father was the only one of their three children born in the USA. He seemed the all-American prototype, a blue-eyed Joe. His name was Joe, I thought, until I saw Guiseppe on his birth certificate! Joe wanted to be a baseball player and made the minor leagues before he was drafted and served as a GI in the second wave at Normandy. While in Europe fighting for our country, some of our Sicilian family was fighting on the other side, the enemy. Later in life, Joe worked in high fashion with Ralph Lauren, a Jewish American from the Bronx. To me both men seemed to be the ultimate Anglo-files creating styles that had a British flair.

I grew up nearly convinced we hailed from England having been educated in English/American schools with a white-washed history of colonial America, knowing little of slaves or Indians or Italian immigrants. Only because of the protests of the 60s did I get a chance to study African/American literature and art at SUNY Albany with an excellent Richard Wright and Jean Toomer scholar, named John Reilly. Yet, the island of Sicily would come to have the greater influence on my unfolding as an adult, artist, spiritualist, and writer. I would discover the why of my call to Africa, to black Madonnas, spiral dances to create modern day rituals that expressed my feminine self. I would learn my Aunt Marion also made a similar journey to Africa to visit our family living in Libya (called Tripoli in 1929), when I discovered a photo of her and her cousin Suzette, dressed in traditional African clothes. I would eventually move to the island of Jamaica, where my Sicilian aunt and her husband migrated to, and later see, after my own trip to Sicily, how much these islands of light resembled each other. My father, who had encouraged my independence as a child, became more authoritarian when I grew up. My mother acted like she personally was in-charge of my virginity. These behaviors came from the old world. Even if I was not born in Sicily, it seemed Sicily still lived in me.

Louisa is the author of the books: *Journey to the Heart Waters* and *In The Eye of Balance*

Chapter 21

I Am Just Like My Sicilian Grandmother

Lauren Sequenzia

My dad has remarked that I was the only grandchild to call his mother something special (the other grandchildren called her grandma) and that I have her Sicilian personality and mannerisms. "Whose girl are you?" my Sicilian grandmother would always ask. We knew it was not a question but more of a statement, a statement of how I was just like her, perhaps? I would blush as if I were shy or something, however we both knew I was not shy, neither was she…and I was just like her. I am not sure who liked this banter of a greeting, every time we encountered, more me or her, but I do know that every time I replied "Gramie's girl" both of our faces lit up. It would usually follow with a huge hug and kiss, and often a pinch of my "fat leggies". I was always big boned like her, probably because we both liked to eat. Christmas was not about presents even when I was a little girl, it was about seeing our family, mostly Gramie, and seeing her vivacious face when we walked through the door.

As a child some of my fondest summer memories were those of normal children, sleep away camps, playing with the neighborhood kids, swimming and biking, however, the memory that sticks out the most was when I spent a few days with my Sicilian Gramie in NJ. Every visit, at a minimum, would always involve sauce and meatballs. She would smush one meatball down in the frying pan until the edges were crunchy and almost burnt, just the way I liked it. And that would be the only snack I could have before we ate. Also included, was her famous homemade Sicilian pizza, hers was the only one I would eat. I have never tasted a sauce like hers since, and no matter how many times I try to replicate her recipe. I have only come close to her sauce once. However, that one time that I came close, was the warmest felt meal I shared with my own family, as I thought of her with every bite! Until I met my husband, I did not really cook much. What I did cook, did not come close to how well my Gramie did. Now that I have a family to cook for, I enjoy cooking and try to do it just as well as my Gramie did, especially the Italian dishes! Eggplant Parmesan is one of my all-time favorites, it is so much work, so I only do it a few times a year, but with each successful batch, I am reminded of her.

My trips to visit Gramie were never complete without a trip to the Point Pleasant, NJ boardwalk. Boy did I enjoy that boardwalk! While most children would beg for money to play endless carnival games and eat cotton candy, all I wanted to do was park my butt in front of a kiddie slot machine and pull that lever repeatedly. My love for slot machines certainly came from Gramie, and probably since she had two real slot machines in her house! I could sit for hours in front of any slot machine, whether it was for quarters or for tokens; it did not matter. Going back to Christmas Eve, the weeks prior we would collect as many quarters as we could, knowing that we would each get a turn to play on Gramie's slot machine the second we arrived. I am extremely fortunate to be the proud inheritor of this slot machine, where the jackpot was three genies for a whopping $37.50 payout! I am so excited for my children and future grandchildren to be able to have similar experiences of excitement on this antique slot machine. The seldom times I find myself at a casino, I always think of her and smile.

Atlantic City…it was about a 45-minute ride from Gramie's house, and that was her favorite place…and my favorite place was anywhere with her! She would get all dolled up, most likely in animal print and oversized earrings. She was such a regular that sometimes we would stay overnight for free. I was so excited for these trips. One would think, what would a young child do in Atlantic City? The lights were mesmerizing. The people watching even better and then I always knew it would involve endless hours in the kiddie casino for tokens and silly prizes at the end. The prizes were just a bonus, the experience was the part I liked most, and watching her, Gramie, in her element of pure bliss…even if she was losing.

I recall the day she passed. I remember being in school and using the payphone to call my dad and ask him to pick me up as I did not want to remain in school. It was like the heart of the family, was ripped out. There would be no more smushed meatballs, or "whose girl, are you?" and no more trips to NJ where her gawdy white leather couches remained. I still remember the hotel we stayed at in Floral Park, NY, when we went to her services. There was no way I was going to allow her to be laid to rest without saying some final words. I believe that I was asked to do a eulogy at her funeral, as many believed that we shared the same outgoing and intense personality. I took this responsibility very seriously, and spent a few hours gathering memories from all her grandchildren to present to the many people who gathered to respect our grandmother being laid to rest.

As I mentioned a few times, Gramie had a vivacious and intense personality, which was also reflected by her choice of décor, clothing, and accessories. I recall going away to college, and I could not go without the largest Sicilian flag that I could find to decorate my side of the dorm room. She was vocal and was not afraid to voice her thoughts... let us just say she and I did not only share the same initials (LEH), but we shared a similar personality. Outspoken, fun, confrontational and loud. Her accessories, the many that she had, were dispersed throughout the family, and while gold jewelry was no longer in style, she had a large gold cursive "L" necklace and ring to match. The monogram was almost 2 inches long! I was given those, not necessarily to wear but as a keepsake of my Gramie. While I do not wear them, I possess them to remind me of how bold and loud she was, just like this jewelry. She was there to make a statement, whether it be out, or with our family, wherever she was. I look forward to passing not only these memories of my Gramie onto my daughter, Lacey, but also this jewelry to go along with it, as she shares the first 2 initials with us as well.

Chapter 22

The Sounds of Silence

Alfred Zappala, Esq.

Why Sicily, Alfred?

Why this obsessive fascination with Sicily that has compelled you to turn your world upside down?

Is it the food? Is it the beauty of the landscape? Is it her rich history? Is it her people? Is it something else?

The questions that I pose today are the very same questions that have rattled in my brain for the last fifteen years.

Every time I think I have an answer, every time I think I know exactly what this magnificent obsession of mine is, something else has come along down the line and thrown my reasoning topsy-turvy.

I have concluded that it is something more fundamental, something more regressive, something that puts me back into a time machine and transports me to a simpler, more secure period of my life.

I think I have a theory now.

Tell me what you think.

A long time ago…in the mid-1950s I think it was, I came to what I call realization of life. In other words, I think I have pinpointed that when I was around five years old or so was the time that I became aware of my surroundings and from this time on in the recesses of my mind life's influences began to register and accumulate.

In other words, I think it was when I was five years old, maybe in 1955 or so, when I actually began to record life's memories in real time so that now, as I rapidly approach geezer- hood, I can hit the rewind switch of life and enjoy and recall the past.

Before that time, my internal memory card had not been properly activated, and whatever I do remember of those very young days does not and did not "stick" with me.

Thus, for the purpose of internal analysis, at age five I came "on-line" so to speak and a visual and recorded life came into my being.

Ok, Alfred…I think I understand where you are going with this. Now, what exactly are you driving at? What are you saying? Clarify, please.

Well, what I can say to you now, what I can relate to you now is this: the sound of background talk is what did it for me… non-understandable background talk… in the Sicilian dialect… spoken by all that loved and nurtured me. This is my ground zero. I remember all the background talk and miss it a lot.

My starting point in life, the essence of my security in life stems from those days of my "extreme" youth, from those days when I was the most vulnerable in life and needed the most protection from the days when feeling secure and loved was the essence of a child's being. This is my nirvana, I think. The reality dawned on me very recently. When, you might ask?

Well, here I am...in my early sixties, a veteran of life's wars and sitting on a bench in Viagrande one warm spring day in May several months back. I found a wonderful little park and I love to stroll around it and think about life. I let the sun beat on my face; I let the smells of the citrus trees and flowers engulf me and I get lost in time and space as I wander.

On one particular day it was the epitome of solitude and quiet. The greenery of the park was intoxicating, the weather comforting, and I had the feeling of complete contentment and happiness as I strolled around my little sacred park. I sat on a bench to relax a bit and closed my eyes to meditate. A group of elderly Sicilian men and women evidently had seated themselves on a bench within earshot of where I sat. I hadn't noticed them.

In the background, I heard the drone of the Sicilian dialect as they chatted while I sat on my bench and relaxed. My mind drifted back in time…far back in time, it seemed.

With the soft drone of the Sicilian dialect in the background from those six wonderful folks who were seated not far from me and talking about everyday life in the Sicilian dialect, I was transported back to my living room on Haverhill Street in Lawrence Massachusetts. And I saw myself… as a five-year-old child.

As I sat on that park bench that day in Viagrande, my memory card of life surged to the "on" position, and I was again a child of five in my childhood living room sitting on the floor playing with my toys while my parents and family talked in the background.

Instead of hearing the voices of the six elderly folks droning on behind me in Viagrande on that warm spring day, I heard the voices of my late father, my late mother, my departed grandparents and my aunt and uncle all speaking in Dialect. The soft inflections of the dialect heard sitting on the bench were the same inflections that I heard long ago. Hearing the ancient Sicilian dialect induced a sense of immense security, contentment, and happiness as it had over half a century ago. That beautiful morning in Viagrande, hearing the soft banter of those six lovely folks had indeed trip-wired my memory recall and transported me back to the epicenter of my being, my existence. The sounds of Sicily today...the ambient sounds of everyday Sicilian life...are and will forever be the cornerstone of my existence. And on this day, this is what I realized. For you see, when I am here in Viagrande I am Alfred. But I am also Santo, Alfio, and Zina, Antoinette, zia Marietta, Uncle Jimmy...and all the voices of long departed loved ones who made me who I am today. They are silenced now as they moved on to a better place but my reason d'être, my reason for being springs from them and from a bygone era. I am grateful to realize this. I have been looking for the answer for a long time and I found it while sitting on a bench in a lovely hill town along the way to Etna. Now, I no longer need to scratch my head and wonder why. Sono Siciliano, that is why. It is who I am.

Reprinted from the book: Joy of My Heart by Alfred Zappala

Alfred is the author of four books about various Sicilian subjects: *The Reverse Immigrant, Gaetano's Trunk, Figghiu Beddu* and *Joy of My Heart*

Chapter 23

"My Maternal Sicilian Family"

Salvatore Liotta

I was born in Beth El Hospital in Brooklyn on May 6, 1949. My mother's family, the Buteras, lived in the Ridgewood section of Brooklyn in a three story, six family brick apartment building across the street from a doll factory on Star Street. My parents lived in a small apartment behind my Uncle Tony's flower shop on Rockaway Blvd. in South Ozone Park at an overpass to the Southern State Parkway. St. Clements's Church, where I became familiarized with Christian iconography, located three streets away. My mother worked in the flower shop. We lived there until I was three years old. My father drove a taxicab at that time. We would visit with my mother's family on Sundays. My Aunt Marie and my Uncle Nicky drove from their home in Howard Beach to Star Street.

My grandmother, Raffaella Bivona, was born in Chiusa Sclafani, a town in central Sicily. I have no idea whether my grandmother's family was related to the original Bivona family. There are Bivonas who emigrated to Rochester. They might have come to Rochester to find jobs with clothier Hickey Freeman. My maternal grandfather was Giuseppe Butera. I have no idea from which town my grandfather emigrated, but I know there is a mountain town in Caltanissetta province named Butera. He might have had been born there. An interesting thing about my grandfather was that Butera for a while was a Muslim town, a Christian town, and a Jewish town. It is possible that I might have had a Jewish family at one time. 10% of Sicilians were Jewish.

Raffaella, my nanna, was my most significant grandparent. I spent much time with her. I lived in her house during three summers when my uncle Peter got me a job working at Rheingold Brewery, and then in construction.

I would drive my grandmother back home to Suffolk County, on the weekends so she could spend time with us in Brentwood, NY. My nanna and I became close. I used to joke with her. "What do I want to study?" she would ask. "Do you want to be a doctor, a lawyer or an engineer?" She heard that being a civil engineer was a good profession, so she specified "civil". She would laugh and call me "scimunitu!" Oftentimes she would call me Giufà. I later learned about Sicilian folk tales in which this "fool" was the central character. She would call me "pupu di zuccaru." I learned what Sicilian I know from my nanna.

Nanna used to give me a quarter and send me off to Knickerbocker Avenue to buy a scalitti which is a blessed loaf of bread. She took me to a chicken market. She would pick out the plumpest chicken she could find. The proprietor would then wring its neck and wrap it up for my grandmother. This I found to be barbaric. This might have set me off toward becoming a vegetarian.

I learned from my grandmother that every drop fills a glass, that first I would suffer, then I would enjoy the fruits of my labor. One night she went to the kitchen sink and let the water drip. In the morning we went to the sink and she showed me a sink filled to the brim with water.

How my *nanna* pounded the message into my head about thrift. After High School I had a job working at Hills Supermarket. I worked 28 hours a week. 4 hours on Monday through Friday evenings and then all day on Saturday. I worked in the supermarket all through my high school years which did not leave much time for study or to have a life beyond work. My starting salary was $1.35 an hour. My ending salary was $1.65 an hour! Every evening I spent the same 27 cents on a bottle of U-Who and a Drake's crumb cake. I thought this was the healthiest snack I could get for 27 cents. When I graduated from High School, I had saved $4,000 toward my tuition. I was proud of this achievement. I always worked hard, and I learned thrift.

There is a legend about my *nanna*. She was given an allowance from my grandfather to purchase groceries and to take care of my mother, her sisters, and my uncle. Out of this allowance she put aside money. She had a plan. She did this for several years. One day my grandparents took a walk. They camc upon two large brick apartment buildings next to each other. My grandmother pointed at one of them and said in Sicilian, "Talè, Talè!". (Look. Look!). Giuseppe grumpily asked: "At what, at what?" My *nanna* said that she had purchased one of the two buildings. Giuseppe was stunned, incredulous. The Buteras left their small apartment on Sydam Street and moved into the large apartment building. It is there where I spent my childhood years with my maternal family.

On the third floor lived my aunt Lillian, Uncle Gary and my cousin Stephen. Another family lived in an apartment down the hall. My aunt Josephine, Uncle Sal, and my cousins Connie and Rae lived on the second floor. Another family lived across the hall. My *nanna* and my uncle Peter lived on the first floor. Down the dark corridor lived a third family which I never saw. There was a door that led down to the basement. I was terrified of who or what might be found at the end of that hall. There was a fourth set of rickety stairs leading to the roof. I was frightened to climb these stairs but climbed them to gaze from the roof at the neighborhood below and the incredible awe-inspiring sight of Manhattan.

Almost every Sunday my mother, father, and sister took the hour drive on the Long Island Expressway so my mother could see her family. Since I commuted to New York Institute of Technology in Old Westbury on the L.I.E., the 495, for my freshman and sophomore years, it seemed that I spent my life on the L.I.E. My Aunt Marie, Uncle Nicky and infrequently my cousins Alfred and Donna would visit with each other on Starr Street in the Ridgewood. All of us would cram into either my Aunt Josephine or my Aunt Lillian's apartment. We sat around a fold-out table which was set up in the living room to eat dinner, the only place that could fit a dozen voluble Sicilians. Caste iron radiators would hiss during the winter. In the spring and summer months windows were open. We ate standard Sicilian foods: spaghetti, meatballs, chunks of beef, sausages, many vegetables, fruit and nuts, maybe even caponata, cardoons, nicely baked cauliflower. On holidays a ham or turkey. The cousins would climb up and down the stairs visiting with one another and eating something in each apartment. Bathroom pipes were used to tap out messages. One time a wonderful thing happened. We were sitting in my aunt Josephine's living room. In the window flew a sparrow which circled around the ceiling and caused a commotion. Out of nowhere my *nanna* jumped up and as fast as Joe Lewis she caught the sparrow, walked to a window and gently released it to its freedom. Everyone else was at a loss. My cousins Connie and Rae screamed. Living amidst ubiquitous brick and concrete, nature was foreign to them. A tiny sparrow could wreak havoc.

Sometimes we got a respite when my Uncle Nick and Aunt Marie would drive out from Howard Beach, Queens to see my mother and father. On rare occasions, my cousin Alfred and Donna would join the large gathering. I was never allowed to stay home and so I thought my cousin Donna and Alfred must have had some kind of special dispensation to be relieved from having to sit in a cramped apartment with and spend the day with family which sometimes spoke Sicilian when they did want nieces and nephews to hear what they were saying. My Uncle Peter would sometimes drive out to Brentwood with my grandmother. We would spend the day on our patio. My father would barbeque lemon garlic chicken on the grill, my mother would make spaghetti, salad, vegetables. Entenmann's was in Brentwood, so we always had pastries, pound cakes, strudels. Sometimes we all met in Howard Beach to spend a Sunday with my Aunt Marie and Uncle Nicky. There was a soundtrack to these Sunday occasions since Howard Beach is just a few miles from Kennedy Airport and therefore, we had to endure the departures and landings of innumerable jets. I received a major influence from my Uncle Nicky. He was a fan of jazz saxophonist Stan Getz. I was in my high school jazz band and loved jazz. Until today, Stan Getz has been my favorite jazz musician. When I lived in Buffalo, and since I have lived in Rochester, I learned that American jazz largely an African American idiom, has had a significant representation of Sicilian Americans. Some notable musicians have been Jimmy Giuffre, Nick La Rocca, Scott La Faro.... I have thought that Sicilians have music in our blood.

Absent from these gatherings was my grandfather, Giuseppe Butera. He never attended any of them. My cabinet maker grandfather's role was mainly that of a specter of the Butera family. My grandfather was a tyrant and an alcoholic. A rare thing for a Sicilian to be an alcoholic. I am not sure how rare it was to be a tyrant. Anyway, decades ago he took a trip back to Sicily. He went back to sell some property. I have no idea where this property was located. My grandfather completed the task. He sold his property. He stuffed his cash in a money belt. He took a Swiss Air flight to return home. The plane crashed on a mountain near Grenoble killing all its passengers. Before my grandfather made his journey, he said that on his return he would make amends for all the suffering that he had caused. He never had a chance to keep his promise to his family.

So along with the lesson of thrift, the value of hard work, and the importance of education that I learned from my grandmother, I learned another important lesson. This one from my grandfather. I learned that individuals could have a powerfully negative as well as a positive impact on the people around them, even their loved ones. He taught me that sometimes in life, time will run out. There might not be any left to try to right a terrible wrong.

I was just two years old when my grandfather was killed. I was too young. I have no clear image of what he looked like. In my nana's dark bedroom. Maybe this darkness was a carryover from living in Sicily where the intense sun made it necessary for homes to have windows shade tightly drawn to keep out the blazing Sicilian sun. In her dark bedroom of her house on there was a large crucifix nailed to the wall. dresser, I used to see a photo of him. standing in a Piazza in Bologna. He was of average height had a dark complexion, and he wore what looked like what was a permanent scowl. I did not get to keep any photo of my grandfather so, indeed; he has been a specter to me. Both my Uncle Peter and I have a resemblance to him. I have always thought that I am mostly a Butera, but should I ever write about Salvatore *numero uno*, my grandfather, you would see that I am also a Liotta.

What Giuseppe Butera was doing in Bologna I never found out. I did learn how my grandfather might have become an angry man, a drunk and a tyrant. Giuseppe's father had a lumberyard, again in some unknown town. The Butera family had a business and wealth. His children were always well dressed in all the photos I have seen. My grandfather wanted to join his friends and study at the University of Bologna, but his father needed his son to help in the family business. He never had a chance to follow his inclination and he never had a chance to make up to his family.

I always thought that my mother's family was haunted because they never spoke about my grandfather. Not ever, except to say that he was an exceedingly difficult man. He would go down to the basement to drink his wine, read, and play his violin which was passed on to me. I thought that my mother's family had circled the wagons. They had closed in on themselves.

I have always wondered whether this was a cultural thing, a family sensibility which resulted from being part of a people whose history has been one long story of foreign invasions, terror, and trauma.

My grandfather offered my uncle Peter the opportunity that his father never had given him, but he refused to take it for one reason or another. I do not know if he ever graduated high school. He wound up finding a job driving a truck for Rheingold Brewery in Brooklyn. My Uncle Peter like his father became an alcoholic but a gentle alcoholic. He was like a second father to me.

Uncle Pete lived with my grandmother in their first-floor apartment on Starr Street. He slept on a single bed which took up a corner of the living room. After work he would return home to eat dinner and to spend time with his family. He would then get restless and would go to spend his evenings at an Italian American social club. There he would socialize. He would get drunk and fall asleep on the couch. When he would awaken, alone. His friends would have gone home to their families. He would drive his Buick Le Sabre and try to get home in one piece.

Uncle Pete's doctor told him he must stop drinking. His blood pressure was dangerously high. His liver was probably in terrible shape. He stopped drinking Scotch but began to drink red wine. One morning my Aunt Lillian find her brother dead on the cold hard subway tile bathroom floor. Stark while porcelain fixtures as cold as death. My uncle was 48 years old. Eventually, my Aunt Lillian found four check books in my uncle's dresser. Uncle Peter had been saving money for years. He paid little or no rent. He was generous with his everyone. He spent little except on alcohol and big cars and left small fortunes to each of his four sisters. My uncle Peter kept asking me if I realized how wonderful our family was. He was always telling me how important it was to be loyal to one's family. Uncle Peter's story is a heart breaker. He loved me and my cousins as if we were his own. He taught me that family was **everything.** One needs family. He used to say "La vita è un pezzu di pani duru." (Life is a piece of hard bread). For him, I guess, it was.

I do not know how representative my maternal Sicilian American family was. Certainly, for the many Sicilian families that have settled in America the Sunday dinners at Grandma's house were a traditional and well-documented experience. The family in the Sicilian American experience was the glue that kept the members for better or worse connected. In every family we have had our share of heartaches, successes and failures, tragedies and joys. But the family somehow made it possible for us to mollify the hard bread of life mentioned by my uncle. We will enter a new phase in the Sicilian American experience when the matriarchs pass away and the togetherness of the family crumbles, letting the diaspora grow in every direction.

PART II

From Our Island

“Think of it (Sicily) as the German Romantic poet Wolfgang Goethe did, who wrote in his diary: *Italy without Sicily leaves no trace upon the soul, Sicily is the key to everything.*”

Reprinted by permission from the book: *What Makes a Sicilian?*, Gaetano Cipolla, Legas, 1996. The original quotation is from W. Goethe's *Viaggio in Italia. (1786-1788),*

Chapter 24

Cannoli: The Gateway to Discovering My Sicilian Heritage

Allison Scola

Some women like going to the jewelry store. I like going to the pastry shop. Perhaps it's a similar sensation: Cases gleaming with works of art of all shapes and sizes that catch your eyes and make your heartbeat faster—at least that's what I experience. Now I know why I love the pastry shop. It's in my DNA. It took many years for me to learn that, but I think I've inherently known it since I was tall enough to see inside the display case.

When I was a child, we lived far from my Sicilian grandmother. She lived in Brooklyn on Avenue X in Gravesend. We lived in Connecticut and then later in Rhode Island. Traveling almost as far as Coney Island to arrive at Grandma's House was a pilgrimage—about two hours in the car, a long ride for a child. I could bare it because as part of that pilgrimage, the reward was a visit to Cuccio's Bakery.

My sweet-tooth comes directly from my father, who, to get to Brooklyn, drove a Ford Pinto with an 8-track tape player that sang classical music or The Beatles (We kids always chose to listen to The Beatles.). No visit to Grandma-in-Brooklyn's house was complete without bringing that white box with the thin red and white string tied around it filled with an assortment of *sfogiatelle*, rum *baba*, Neapolitans, and of course, cannoli.

Growing up, I thought all Americans ate cannoli for every holiday. I may have been in college when I learned that cannoli were an Italian American thing and not an American thing. That was news to me.

When we lived in Rhode Island during my teenage years, my father complained about the cannoli in Providence. "They don't taste like the ones from Brooklyn," he would say. And when he asked the pastry shop what the baker put in the cream, they told him ricotta and mascarpone cheese. Needless to say, we didn't eat too many cannoli in Rhode Island.

While backpacking through Europe in 1996, I contacted my father's first cousin, Pietro, who was a pastry chef in Rome. I had never met him and his wife Maria, who came to visit me at the convent in the city center where I was staying. They were excited to meet me, his American-cousin Peter's daughter. Pietro and Maria brought with them a tray of pastries from his shop. I still remember that beautiful collection of jewels and how I savored each one over the subsequent days. I didn't speak Italian at the time, only musical terms, so another backpacker helped translate our conversation.

Pietro spoke fondly about my grandmother, Lorenzina and my father's visits to Sicily as an eight-year-old in 1950 and during 1964 when he was studying in Rome. But when he spoke about Sicily, he waxed poetic.

He asked me about my travel plans and responded, "You're not going to Sicily?"

I had my Grand Tour of Europe already planned, and I didn't know anything about Sicily—nor did it occur to me to go there. I was traveling alone, and without having command of Italian language, I didn't think it was possible. It seemed so far away and hard to navigate.

Pietro was disappointed. Still, his description of his brothers and nieces and nephews in this exotic place—my cousins—piqued my curiosity. So did his delicious cannoli.

After our encounter, I headed north to Florence, Bologna, Venice, through the Alps, and on to Salzburg and Vienna during which on every train ride, I studied Italian. I had fallen in love. In love with Italy, in love with Italian, and in love with Italians. I traveled through Germany and France and Spain and back to the United Kingdom, where I had lived and worked in London for six months leading up to this adventure. I couldn't shake the feeling that Italy was where I was meant to be.

When my money ran out, I flew home to the States to earn and save more in order to return. Five months later, in September 1996, I was back in Rome, suckling on a *cannolo* in Pietro's shop, Conco D'Oro in the Finocchio neighborhood of the city. I hit the pavement seeking work, yet after two weeks failing to gain under-the-table employment in the Eternal City, I regretfully decided it was time for me to return home. Pietro said, "You're not leaving for America without going to Sicily first."

To my amazement, insisting, he picked up the phone and called his older brother Mimmo to say I was arriving the next night at Palermo's central train station.

During the 12-hour journey, my *Ferrovie dello Stato Italiane* train snaked its way down the Italian peninsula. After Naples, Salerno, and Reggio Calabria, it was disassembled and reassembled to cross the Strait of Messina. We then traversed 140 miles across the north coast of Sicily. Seven minutes before we were to arrive in Palermo, I realized I had not yet considered how I might find my unfamiliar cousins. I panicked.

I was arriving at ten o'clock at night in the train station of an infamously Mafia-ridden city—a 24-year-old, single, American woman who spoke about 500 words of Italian mostly in the present and past tenses.

Deep breaths.

"I've been all over Europe by myself. I can do this," I thought.

I grabbed my backpack and climbed down the train's stepladder to the platform. Within a moment I saw faces of two older gentlemen who I immediately recognized. They possessed sharp cheek bones, kinky hair, and thin arms similar to those of my grandmother's back in Brooklyn. I knew I belonged to them.

"Al-Y-zon?" They asked, transforming my American name into their tongue.

For the next three weeks, I was immersed in a foreign, but familiar world. I met a clan of loving, animated cousins, including my second-cousin Evelina, who was six months younger than me. Every day I was exposed to the treasures of Palermo and its surroundings. Monreale Cathedral, the church, and cloisters of San Giovanni degli Eremiti, Sicily's Regional Art Museum at Palazzo Abatellis, and the ficus tree at Piazza Marina. We broke through the language barrier and grew very close. I ate caponata and *panelle* and *arancine*—which I hadn't ever tasted before. And I ate out-of-this-world cannoli.

During that visit, I learned more about my great uncle Dominic who my father had mentioned periodically during my childhood. *Zio Domenico* owned Bar Aurora, a renowned café, *pasticceria,* and *gelateria* on the Corso Umberto I in Bagheria. In the summer of 1950, when my father was eight and running freely around town, it was there that he spent afternoons sucking on gelato and watching the *ragazzi* work in the kitchen. In 1996, during my first visit to Sicily, Bar Aurora was no longer the hotspot it had been in the years after World War II. It has since closed, and now, when I tell people in Sicily of my relationship to it, they sing its praises. It is as if I come from royalty.

My cousin Pietro, who spent his early years learning his craft at Bar Aurora before going to professional pastry school in Palermo and then moving to Rome, together with my cousin Mimmo, now in his eighties and who also worked in the *laboratorio* as a teenager, are significant sources for how I make cannoli and explain it to all who listen. For example, Pietro taught me to blend the ricotta, confectioners' sugar, and vanilla extract, wrap it in cheesecloth, and then let it rest overnight to allow even more whey to drain from it. And Mimmo explained that for the shell, use lard. Lard in the pastry dough and lard for frying. This, in addition to a blend of marsala wine and wine vinegar, is what makes the shell crispy and light.

Importantly though, I learned what makes Sicilian cannoli distinct from the American cannoli I grew up savoring. The principal difference: the ricotta. In Sicily, most of the island uses sheep's milk ricotta versus here in the United States, where we exclusively use cow's milk ricotta. The divergence originates from the availability of ingredients. At the turn of the 20th-century, Sicilian immigrants in the United States could not source sheep's milk, so they turned to cow's milk and proceeded to flavor the ricotta, aiming to emulate the natural sweetness of sheep's milk. They added cinnamon and candied orange, lemon, and citron, for example. Americans then became accustomed to this recipe. Note that when tasted side by side, the taste has an obvious difference.

Now, after spending years visiting my cousins and traveling throughout Sicily and eating dozens of cannoli, it has become a mission of mine to explain this distinction. What I've learned though, is that it isn't just about pastry. It's about identity.

Through cannoli, I've discovered my heritage—my heritage as a Sicilian American. Because like the cow's-milk ricotta-based cannoli sold at Cuccio's in Brooklyn, I was raised with a blueprint that was based in something traditional, yet my culture and way of life has been transformed by place and time. Yes, I have a lot in common with my cousins in Bagheria—kinky, thick hair, defined cheekbones, and strong emotions. We definitely belong to each other; yet we possess essential differences that make them Sicilian and me American. And the result, is something to appreciate, enjoy, and celebrate—like a good cannolo.

Allison Scola is owner/curator of Experience Sicily, a boutique tour operator, and founder of the Cannoli Crawl, a walking and food tour in New York City.

Chapter 25

Somewhere in Time in Sicily (Childhood Experiences of Sicily by an Immigrant from Sicily)

Serafino Pace

U Cantaturi Sicilianu (The Sicilian Storytellers)

During the summer season, a few storytellers would come to my town. They were the Sicilian actors at a time when there was no theater, playing the parts of a story in the center of town. They would show large pictures and would describe the story with poems and songs while playing along with the guitar or accordion. One story was about D'Artagnan and the Three Musketeers (Athos, Porthos, and Aramis). Another was about King Arthur, Camelot, and the English Knights. But the one story that would attract most of the local people, including myself, was the story of "Turiddu Giulianu" (Salvatore Giuliano).

It was a true story that happened in Sicily at the end of the war. The story was about a young man who, when he was eighteen years old, took care of his sick and starving mother. At that time, he tried to steal a bag of wheat and was caught by a Carabiniere (Policeman). He tried to escape and, instinctively, pushed the Carabiniere down some steps where he hit his head very hard on the ground, dying on the spot. Scared and afraid of the consequences, he ran away to the mountains, which surrounded his town of Montelepre.

Although very young, Turiddu was very smart while hiding in the mountains and was able to elude the searches by the police. In the following months, many other desperate and jobless young people joined him. He soon became a Sicilian folk hero, protecting people in need. He would steal from the rich and give it all to the poor, like a modern-day Robin Hood. But Turiddu Giulianu's real dream was to see Sicily become independent from the rest of Italy. That's not what the Italian politicians wanted to hear. They conspired against him, paying a large amount of money to one of his cousins to kill him. He was shot dead at the age of twenty-nine while on his way to speak to the Sicilian Assembly in Palermo, in hopes that they would back him up in the separation of Sicily from the rest of Italy. In my own way, I'll try to write some of the singing and the poetic melody that described his short life:

Vi cantu la storia di lu briganti Turiddu
(I'll sing the story of the outlaw Turiddu)
Ca pi un saccu di farina la leggi arrestau
(That for a bag of wheat he was arrested)
Cercannu di scappari, un Carabiniere forti ammutau
(Trying to escape, he pushed a policeman with all his strength)
Sbattennu la testa nterra lu Carabiniere muriu.
(The policeman died when he hit his head on the ground)
Lu picciutteddu tuttu scantatu
(The young man was scared)
Di cursa nta la muntagna fui scappatu
(Running as fast as he could, he escaped into the mountains)
Pi journa e journa la leggi lu circau
(For days and days the police searched for him)
Tutti li parti di li muntagni e nun l'attruvau
(Up into the mountains without finding him)

...And that's the way it was somewhere in time in Sicily.

The Old Ways

Many years ago, when I was very young, somewhere in time in Sicily, right after the end of World War II, things were different than today's life. In the small town where I grew up, and in the house where I was born, life was simple and very fulfilling. As young kids, my two older brothers and I did not ask for much, and we were not getting much, but every little thing that we got was the world to us. Life was very difficult, with many people looking for jobs. On the day that I was born, the weather was miserable (not that I remember any of it) with heavy winds and lots of rain. January is one of the coldest months of the year anyway. At that time, births were performed in people's houses with the help of a midwife. They were very capable women, with lots of experience and knowledge. But the truth of the matter was only a few people were able to afford the hospital and the doctor's bill. The house where I was born was a split-level home. There were two rooms on the first floor and a bathroom with a shower. On the second floor, there was one large bedroom with a balcony. My mother told me, when I was old enough to understand, that they bought the house at the price of two thousand lira. After many years of working on people's properties, my father and mother were able to save one thousand lira, and they used it as a deposit for the house, and the other thousand they got through a mortgage from the local bank. My mother had an older sister, Rosa, and every day we would visit her, some days more than once. Mom told me during one of our visits that Rosa's house was the house that she grew up in. The house was originally Grandma's house, before her older daughter Rosa got married, as it was a common thing at the time that the first daughter would receive the house as a price for the wedding, and the rest of the family would move out. My grandmother moved out with my mother from the place she had known all her life into a rented two-room apartment. When it was my mother's turn to find a husband, at eighteen years old, a few young men were interested in her, but they balked at the knowledge that she had nothing to offer for the marriage. But not my father. He didn't care about property or money, he was in love with her, and he married her the way she was.

And that's the way it was somewhere in time in Sicily.

Remembering Life in Sicily

Sicily's main resource was always agriculture. There weren't many factories to employ people. All the extra jobs were connected with working in the fields, taking care of animals or selling fruit or vegetables that would grow almost everywhere.

When you are poor, you'll do almost anything for extra money. For us kids growing up, it was very difficult finding jobs but, if you were willing to work, there were some odd jobs around. One of those jobs was located a block away from my house. The owner of a large property would set up a table in front of his house with many chairs around it where most of us kids would sit. He would fill the table with many bushels of "mennuli" (almonds), with the original green skin attached after taking them down from the trees. The way that it was done was very simple. The branches of the tree were shaken violently, knocking down the mennuli onto a large plastic sheet on the ground. Our job was to take off their green skin so they could be sold to the stores. After every bushel of mennuli were cleaned, we would get paid a few lira.

Another odd job was to help set up "la ricotta cu lu seru" (ricotta with juice). The owner of sheep at the end of the town needed help to carry the milk from the sheep to a small barn where he already set up a large pot over a fire. After the milk boiled for a while, the ricotta would rise to the top. Some days there were over twenty people waiting in line to buy his ricotta. The owner would scoop up some of the ricotta and put it in containers with some of the juice (that had a sour taste) from the pot and charge a few lira. The combination of the sweet ricotta and the sour juice and fresh bread would create an amazing taste. That's one of the many things that I miss about Sicily.

But one memory that stands out the most in my mind was the memory of this person that, every Saturday morning on a "carretto Siciliano" full of potatoes, would come to our street and from the top of his lungs would scream: "Patate, patate, chi mangia patate non muore mai!" (Potatoes, potatoes, whoever eats potatoes will never die!) From my father I found out that this man had a small potato farm where he would work from Monday to Friday. On Saturday he would sell them, traveling through the streets of our town.

Many times, when my kids were a little too picky with the vegetables or the food my wife and I would make for them, I would repeat the famous phrase: "Patate, patate, chi mangia patate non muore mai!"

And that's the way it was somewhere in time in Sicily.

Guardie e Ladri (Guards and Thieves)

As a youngster growing up in a small town, you knew many people and had lots of friends. Most of my friends were kids on my block and in my neighborhood. On summer nights, we would gather near our favorite corner building on Main Street where the streetlights were very bright, playing street games. We didn't have TVs, CD players, phones, or any other fancy toys; we only had each other. Playing in the street was the only thing available to us. The game we enjoyed playing the most was "Guardie e Ladri" (Guards and Thieves). It was a very simple game. Everybody got a card from a playing deck and the two lowest cards became the guards, while everyone else became a thief. After counting to ten, the guards began to chase the thieves, until they would catch one of them by tagging any part of their body. The thief would be taken to the corner of the building where one of the guards would stand and the other would continue his search for the others. Eventually, one by one, all the thieves would become prisoners and the game would be over. But if one of the thieves, before he got caught, touched the hand of one of the prisoners that were standing on the corner, all of them would be free to run again. The game would go on until late at night, or when our mothers would start calling us to go home.

One very warm night, in the middle of July, we were playing our usual game of "Guardie e Ladri." The guards that night were two brothers, Tony and Giovanni. We all started running when being chased by them, but soon we were all exhausted because of the very hot and humid night. Instead of running, we started hiding here and there. At the end of the evening, some mothers started calling their kids home: "E tardi, tutti a casa!" (It's late everyone go home!) We all started getting out of our hiding places and started going home, except for Salvatore. He was very cozy in his hiding spot, and with the hot and humid night, he fell asleep. Sometime later in the middle of the night, the whole neighborhood got woken up. Salvatore's parents were banging on everyone's doors, looking for their son. We all started running out into the street, calling and looking for him. "Salvatore, Salvatore!" yelling as loud as we could. His mother was hysterical crying, afraid that something terrible had happened to him. Other mothers started crying too, feeling sorry for her and concerned for Salvatore's wellbeing. Finally, all the screaming and yelling woke Salvatore up. Confused and still half asleep, he appeared from his hiding place, saying "What? What's happening?" staring at the crowd of people in the street. Before anyone could answer him, his mother ran over to him, followed by his father. They were all over him, kissing and hugging him, while his mother was still crying. Everyone moved in and made a circle around them. A few minutes later Salvatore and his parents started walking home, holding each other. The rest of us stayed there a few moments, watching them walk away, until we started walking back to our homes. The streets once again became quiet and peaceful.

And that's the way it was somewhere in time in Sicily.

The Circus

Once a year, almost at the same time every year, a small circus would come to my town for two weeks. The circus owner was a man in his 50's and was married with a family that consisted of three daughters and four sons. Besides the family members, there were five men and four women to complete the rest of the circus crew. It was a very small circus, without tigers or lions or elephants. The largest animals were horses. They also had two monkeys, a small bear and a few trained dogs.

All the kids in town were always excited to see his tent erected in one of the empty lots. I would do anything my parents would tell me to do in the two weeks that the circus was in town. I would also be very well behaved in school, hoping to have the chance to see the circus at least once. I was fascinated at the thought of it, thinking of all the traveling they do all over Sicily, enjoying the beautiful things that only Sicily has to offer. For days after it was gone, I would still imagine myself living that magical and glamorous life, feeding the animals, playing around with the clowns, and swinging on the trapeze.

Once there was an empty lot across the street from my house and one year the circus parked their tent there. With my father's help, they were able to set up the electricity and water connections. For that favor, the owner of the circus gave my brothers and I a pass to see the circus any time we wanted, and we were also free to walk around and feed the animals with the trainers. This was a blessing for me. I was so excited that I couldn't sleep at all that night. I waited by the window for the sun to rise so I could finally walk across the street and be part of the daily circus life. From that moment on I spent every free minute walking around the animal cages and the circus people's living quarters.

But after three or four days of being part of it and seeing how hard everyone worked all day, my magic balloon quickly burst! Watching them practicing for their act or training the animals for hours and hours every single day was, to me, a bit boring and depressing. They struggled to survive at a period of time when many people were out of work, and their fatigued bodies had no medical relief. But at night when it was showtime, everyone would force a smile on their face. After all, "The Show Must Go On!" This was the time in my life when I learned that all that glitters isn't gold.

And that's the way it was somewhere in time in Sicily.

Chapter 26

On the Street of Lights

Marisa Frasca

Peter and I put English on pause and began conversing with each other in our native language once the plane approached Catania. I caught the full sight of Etna rising like a dark sun. Alitalia's 747 landed and I got down on hands and knees to kiss the concrete of Fontanarossa's airport—from the sheer joy of stepping foot on native ground again. My husband gave me a strange look as I recall. But this was a time for wistful affection. Twelve long years had passed, and I was returning to my island. I was on my honeymoon and eager to introduce my husband to my beloved aunt and uncle and my first cousins. I promised myself to look up a few childhood friends I'd lost touch with. Would I recognize any of them?

The airport was behind us but again I gave myself away as a sentimental fool on the two-hour drive from Catania to Vittoria. In a rented Fiat 500, our luggage tied to the roof, I pleaded with Peter to stop the car when I saw a tree heavy with fruit. The landscape was spotted with farmhouses and cows. You could pick a bouquet of fifty different wildflowers on the road to Camerina that led us closer to Vittoria, my hometown. On the side of the road we bought a watermelon from a street vendor's pull-cart brimming with watermelons. *Muluni, Muluni*, the street vendor sang in his Vittorese drawl. Watermelon, watermelon—pulp for eating and rind to polish your shoes, the street vendor said.

What Hallelujahs greeted us when we arrived at our destination and my aunt and uncle could not stop crying, could not stop embracing me as if I had miraculously come back from the dead. We had regularly kept in touch by telephone since I was ten years old. My mother made sure of it from the day we arrived in America. Long distance phone calls were costly back then but as necessary as bread, at least once every few months we needed to hear familial voices.

Aunt Gina finally settled down and showed us around the house

I remembered. She opened the door to her bedroom and insisted that Peter and I unpack our things. On her dresser were photographs my photographer father had taken of my cousins and I playing at the beach. I stomped my feet like a child trying to dissuade my aunt from giving up her bedroom. All the while I was admiring the bed so beautifully dressed in white hand-embroidered sheets and matching coverlet. I made the gesture of pulling my hair out in protest. We could sleep on the sofa bed in the living room. My cousins said give it up; you know there is no arguing with your aunt Gina. She made up your bed three days before you arrived.

There was no arguing with my cousins either. Paolo and Maria Giovanna took two weeks off from work even though it was not yet August when all of Italy shuts down for holiday. I sat with my extended family before a banquet of food my aunt prepared each day, delicious beyond words. After our main meal some of us filed inside our rooms for afternoon naps. My grandmother played solitaire in the courtyard after shelling tomorrow's pea. Peter woke first and nudged her to play a game of *Scopa* instead. I listened to my cousin Paolo strumming his guitar. Some days we took the guitar along on day trips to the beach and nearby Noto and Ragusa. We were all back in Vittoria by evening for our customary walk on Via Cavour, dubbed *A Strata e Lumi*, The Street of Lights, open only to foot traffic, just the way I remembered. No cars. No motorbikes.

On the Street of Lights was the remarkable and unremarkable life of the townspeople—a swarm of men and women of all ages, as well as teenagers and children exchanging pleasantries before speculating and arguing, *Buona Sera, Prego, Dopo lei* (after you). Who do you think will win the world cup? I wish Italy would buy Pele`. Why Pele` when we have our own soccer legends? Did you watch the San Remo festival on TV this year? They call that music? Bring back Adriano Celentano's legs all sparks and dazzle like Elvis, not long-face De Gregori. Those nose-up-in-the-air Northern Italians will swear that De Gregori is a poet. A poet? What's he mumbling about? Trains half empty and half full. *Merda. Che schifo!*

For the night ahead was another evening walk and I might overhear a conversation about the *Littorina* (Vittoria's train). How it was never on time when you most needed it. How sometimes it was standing room only. Shrinking time schedules. One woman whined about the train being a cesspool and a how a dirty old man took advantage of the train's jerking motion. He got a little too close. She was mortified all the way to Palermo. Another woman revealed herself unguarded: "I was with you. I didn't see you draw back. And the man was not that old." On the Street of Lights, you moved while overhearing snippets of a stranger's life—marital complications, conflicts with children, who said what to whom, and always the financial woes. Little had changed since I was a girl. Then again, memory becomes distorted by time.

Again, I walked arm-in-arm with members of my family and I suppose I was reflected in them. My husband said we looked like battle chargers taking up the width of the street. Occasionally he let go of my arm to enter a coffee bar and attempt to offer us an aperitif, pastries, gelato, whatever each of us preferred. I can still hear the friendly fight erupting between Peter and my uncle Giovanni. One man shoving and shouting at the other for the privilege of picking up the tab, and even before that, two extra ricotta *cassateddi,* perfectly wrapped in case my sweet tooth kicked in later, in case my grandmother at home hadn't yet gone to sleep and needed a snack. Such mad love was in the air that summer of '73.

We strolled and reached the end of the street that opened to the Piazza and the Villa beyond, took a few moments to sit on a park bench near thick low scrubs, uncultivated vegetation that survived in endless dust, that had a silence you could almost hear, that followed you heading back in the opposite direction, towards home. While I smiled at strangers and familiar faces in this interconnected world I loved, I kept thinking where is home for the immigrant? I entered Italy as a tourist and will re-enter America as an alien with papers. I often lost my heart under the cobblestones on the Street of Lights. Perhaps the air itself rained messages all those years ago and it was then I understood the somber suffering of immigrants who have not quite died in the old country and have not yet been born in the new. How we fly back and forth like the osprey's need to return to its birthplace.

I have been back to Sicily more than a dozen times since my first return but have never been as constantly teary-eyed as I was then. Always caught somewhere between happiness and sadness on those evening walks while one or another of my loved ones dragged me in and out of cafés, tasting *nocciola, granita al limone con brioche,* and Aunt Gina planting kisses on my face: *Amore mio,* how I loved to watch you snuggle in bed between your uncle and me when you were little. *Sangu mio,* (my blood) you're so beautiful in that dress but if you're set on wearing it again tomorrow night let me at least iron it. I'm still laughing at the thought of my aunt Gina wanting to save me from the wrinkles, and God forbid the neighbors' gossip. If the aunt I adored, still adore, wanted to weave stiff bamboo into my linen dress and lose the fashionable wrinkles I'd paid good money for in America, who was I to argue?

I was rejoicing in florid melodrama and taking photos of even the common pigeon searching for breadcrumbs on The Street of Lights. My childhood friend, Anna, might have said: Marisu`, you've turned into that Dumb American with camera around the neck we used to snub when we were kids. How ruthless my friend Anna could be? Of course, then as now I only speculate about what Anna might have said. On the Street of Lights, the street of joys and sorrows, I learned that Anna died shortly after my parents and I left for America. Anna who throbbed with dream while she ran out of Sunday Mass like a pony with free-flowing hair, Anna whom I walked with, hip to tender hip, and Anna who impersonated Arethusa, Sicily's most beloved Goddess. I forget now which Goddess I was when we played statuettes on The Street of Lights and Anna and I anticipated life to come and forgot to be mortally small.

Marisa Frasca is the author of two books: *Via Incanto: Poems from the Darkroom* and *Wild Fennel: Poems and other Stories*

Chapter 27

Coming to America

Anthony Malatino

This piece is the story of a young woman, my mom. She was born in Albany, New York, the oldest of six children and lived there until she was 11 years old. Her parents, in 1922, decided to move the family back to their homeland Sicily. My mom spent most of the next 27 years in a desperate attempt to return to the land she loved.... America. I was fortunate enough to share her experience. This story is neither sad nor unique. In post-WWII Sicily they were many stories of struggles and triumphs. This is simply one of many.

I was born in Sicily in a small town at the base of Mount Etna. My family's journey to America started when I was six years old. I have often said over the years that "I am one of the luckiest people in the world" having grown up in post-World War II America when all things were possible. Every few years I travel back to Sicily to visit with my relatives. Both Mom and Pa came from large families, so gatherings are usually 50 to 60 people. It helps that I can still manage to speak a little Sicilian.

My mom was the oldest of six children born in Albany, N Y to Antonino and Carmella Vecchio. They lived in the "Italian" section of town. Grandpa "Nino" worked as a groundskeeper at the Albany Country Club, one of the oldest in the country, dating back to the 1890s. Later in in life I remember him often talking about the tennis courts he maintained. My grandmother, who died before I was born, managed the small boarding house they owned. Together they did well financially.

Grandma Carmella never really liked living in such a cold climate. She came to America in 1908 to marry my grandfather and spent most of the next fourteen years pregnant, not unusual in those days. I am told that she lost several more children as infants or due to miscarriages.

In 1922 she convinced my grandfather to move back to Sicily. They had accumulated quite a bit of money for those days. My grandpa loved horses and the idea of starting a carriage trade back in the old town appealed to him.

1922 the Vecchios sailed back to "the old country", my mom was devastated. She was 11 years old, loved America, her friends and school. She admitted being one of the brightest students.

In Sicily, grandpa bought several horses and carriages and started his "taxi" service carrying passengers to and from the small neighboring towns, the train station and of course the almost weekly funerals. Life expectancy was not high in Sicily back then. Sixty was considered old.

For years things seem to be working out well. The old family house on the main street was large and comfortable with a spectacular view of Mount Etna, and the weather in a small town at 3,000 feet elevation was almost nearly perfect... good air and water.

It was not so perfect for my mother, however since her Italian was limited, she was placed in the second or third grade with seven and eight-year-olds. She recalled how embarrassing it was.

Taking care of her younger siblings (two more were born in Sicily) became a larger and larger role ... life was not as joyful as it was in America.

The worldwide depression of the 1930s was especially hard in Sicily, which was already poor to begin with. Grandpa's business failed. The horses and carriages had to be sold for whatever could be had. From that time on, life was a daily struggle. At twenty-four years old, mom married my father after eloping. Many couples eloped back then for any number of reasons, not the least of which was that they were too humiliated to admit they had no money for a proper wedding. The girl's family always protested the elopement vigorously as shameful and degrading, while quietly breathing a sigh of relief.

Mom recalled my father and her knocking on the local priest door early one morning asking to be quickly married. The priest obliged but said that they needed a witness and it was early in the morning. My father went outside found the street sweeper and presto... a witness! My mom sadly but jokingly would recall "there we were the Bride, the Groom and the broom".

After the birth of their first child named Graziella, mom and my father a shoemaker by trade, made plans to emigrate to America. Mom was American, never having relinquished her citizenship.

Unfortunately, that was not meant to be as her mother died the same year. No one knows exactly what she died from, but she had twenty-two births. Eight children lived. My mom, as the oldest, was obliged to take care of her younger siblings. Her father was so despondent at losing his livelihood and his wife that he became another one to care for. Within a year of marrying, my parents inherited a family of 10, all this with no appreciable income. The American dream had instantly evaporated.

My parents scratched out a living through the first-floor store at the front of the house. Nothing special, just whatever they could find to sell. From tomatoes and broccoli to some of the upstairs furniture, whatever it took. My brother Joseph was born a few years later and their daughter Graziella died at five years old due to the flu. I was born a few years later.

By then, Italy was in World War II, allied with Germany. Not only was America no longer an option, but American born citizens like my mom and her siblings had to keep a low profile.

The war years, with so many months mouths to feed, were an unimaginable challenge for this young couple. The two oldest boys were drafted into the Italian military. Citizenship did not matter. In fact, the two boys were instructed not to speak of their American birth. One died somewhere in Sardinia without a trace. The other made it home after the war. He walked for 10 days to reach home.

With the war finally over mom wasted no time trying to prove her American citizenship and that she wanted to return to the USA. Her younger sisters were now old enough to take care of the rest of the family until she and my father could earn enough to send for them.

By 1949, mom was able to borrow enough money to book passage for herself and my older brother Joseph, who like my mother, was considered American citizen since he was born to an American citizen prior to Italy entering World War II against the allies. Unfortunately, I was not an American citizen. Mom could not have taken me anyway. My brother at nine years old could go to school while she worked. At five, I would have to wait until she earned enough money to send for my father and me. Also, making applications for my father and me took some time. A year later my father and I left our small town in Sicily and I began my incredible American journey.

Things are so different today that I find myself saying, as I recall those days, "really can it be, did that really happen?"

When we arrived at the dock in Palermo, my father was quickly advised that I was not allowed in the same cabin as he. His was for adult men and I was to be in a children's cabin. There was no arguing. Then, out of the blue, as my father recalls, a stranger approaches my father with a young boy, 12 years old I believe and begged my father to look after the boy on the ship as he was traveling by himself. I am not sure what the arrangement was, but my father agreed. How could he say no? My father did insist that the boy be in the same cabin as me. I kept the passport my father and I traveled on and sure enough a small written statement next to my father's name lists him as the guardian for this previously unknown young person, amazing! We were escorted to the children's cabin where there were bunkbeds for six. At my young age I had little choice of beds. Other than the train from my small town to Palermo, I had never been on anything that moved. My grandfather's donkey is the only exception.

The moment they untied the ship lines on the dock, I got seasick. The trip was 11 days and I was nauseous continuously. If I weighed 50 pounds when I left Palermo; I was less than 40 pounds upon arrival in New York. The nightmare of the voyage finally ended in early November. We sailed towards New York Harbor in the early morning, the first calm waters in many days. I rushed on deck to witness what to this day, is the most incredible, wondrous sight I have ever seen. There was no Verrazano Bridge at the time. The curvature of the earth had the Manhattan skyline simply rising from the water and on one side this enormous statue of the lady holding a torch also rising slowly.

As we entered the harbor, I was amazed at the number of boats in the water flying red, white, and blue flags. Even the great statue was draped in an American flag. Those on the boats were all waving at us. I thought "look what they are doing for us on our arrival". I loved it. It was only a few years later that I realize that all the hoopla was because it was November 11, Veterans Day! The happiness and joy I felt instantly erased all the pain and suffering from the long voyage. Mothers holding their newborn infants attest to that, I am told.

As we as we pulled closer to our pier on the west side of Manhattan, the wonders intensified. Everything was big, so many things moving, so busy. I am sure I had to be holding on to something, because to this day, when I think of it my heart races.

The rest was a blur of passengers and luggage and loudspeakers. We finally walked down the ramp to the pier. Our steamer trunk and luggage were waiting on the pier floor. I remember the night before we were to arrive, we were told to place our luggage outside our cabins. That morning the ship's crew placed stickers with the letter M on our items, the first letter of our last name. Before we were permitted to disembark all luggage was on the pier under overhanging signs corresponding with the first letter of the passenger's last name. Pretty neat and organized I thought. It made an impression on me as Palermo was not so organized.

My mother was waiting at the street side of the pier behind a barricade. It was a typical customs situation. Eventually we cleared customs and we all kissed and cried. I am not sure if I cried as I was still in amazement. Then more amazement. Our luggage was wheeled out and we proceeded towards the biggest automobile I have ever seen or imagined. A kindly old gentleman in a suit helped my father load the trunks and bags into this thing and off we went. Before I realized, he was driving on a street that was "in the air". Today, whenever I drive to New York City, across the George Washington Bridge and make my way down the elevated portion of the West Side Highway, it is November 11 all over again.

I do not remember much about the long ride to Albany. The Thruway (I- 87) did not exist then. It was the two-lane Route 9. With all the excitement, I probably fell asleep. Days later, I would realize that enormous automobile which easily held on our steamer trunk and luggage was a hearse. My mother had hired the hearse from the local funeral home. The Italian funeral director rented his hearse for picking up relatives arriving from Italy. Years later, I would think back and smile as I arrived at my new home and life in a hearse. For many, the only ride in a hearse is at the end of their life. For me, it was the beginning of a wonderful journey. My mom eventually brought her brothers and sisters back to America, as she promised. She lived to be 95. While she maintained many of the Sicilian traditions, she loved every minute of her life in America.

Chapter 28

An Emotional Homecoming to my Ancestral Village in Sicily

Mark Hehl

Below is an edited chapter from the book – An Immigrant's Dilemma, *which shows some of the differences and similarities between family and social events in Sicily and North America.*

My wife and I arrived at Santa Margherita di Belice (AG) on April 24, 2017 so that final research for *An Immigrant's Dilemma* could be completed. I was interested in connecting with the Sicilian descendants of my great-grandfather and finding out why he left America without all but one of his children. My plan was to interview some older family members who could answer my questions, then perform some research at the town hall. Shortly after arriving, my cousin Peppino indicated that the following day was a holiday and consequently, the town hall would be closed. April 25 is Liberation Day, a national holiday in Italy. It marks the fall of Mussolini's Italian Social Republic and the end of the Nazi occupation of Italy in 1945.

At first, I was disappointed because of losing valuable research time; however, this proved to be a bonus for me. On this day, Sicilians have large family gatherings usually outside their town, at small villas owned by family member or friends. Peppino built one such villa and hosted the event at his villa. He did not give us any advance information on what was to occur or where we were going. He just said to be ready at 11 AM and that he would come to fetch us. We followed him and were surprised to discover the bonus that was planned.

We entered the complex and began to meet those already there, mostly my relatives. My wife, Olga, had the task of being my interpreter that day. Her Italian was a bit rusty, but it improved as the day progressed.

The complex contained a swimming pool, lemon trees and three outdoor wood ovens (no gas grills here). One oven was built just for pizza. There was a wind turbine; Peppino sells the excess generated power to the electric company. The hot water was solar-heated. He had a well and cistern, all of which made the villa self-sufficient. We Americans can learn from this.

Upon our arrival, the intense preparations were under way. The men were attending to the outdoor woodburning ovens. The women were in the kitchen washing and chopping the vegetables and fruits. My wife Olga also began to help by preparing some strawberries. This was an opportunity for her to learn more about Sicilian cooking.

The first thing I noticed was that the pizza oven was already going, along with one other outdoor oven. The pizza oven had some grape vine wood burning just to heat it up for use later that day. The group was preparing the first course, cipollini con porchetta (pork strips wrapped in scallions), cooked over a wood fire in the other outdoor oven. The smell of the cooking pork and charred wood told me that I was in for some delightful food. I was right.

We then had a spaghetti course with a tomato-tuna-basil sauce, where the sauce was not cooked (a bit different to what I was used to growing up in an Italian-American household). It would not have been an Italian meal without at least one pasta course. Later, the men cooked some sausage and eggplant slices on the same open fire, with a slightly different delightful aroma of pork, spices and burning wood. These tasted very much like the Italian sausages in the USA, with the wood fire giving it some added smoky flavor. They also served caponata, an eggplant based salad, which took me back to my childhood. I had not eaten caponata since my childhood and said to my wife: "This tastes like Brooklyn". It caused me to think about my youth spending many Sunday afternoons at my great uncle Edward's (born Ignazio) house at Brooklyn's Halsey Street, where the extended family gathered. This trip back in time was one of the many emotional moments of that day. All of this went well with some local white wine produced in the neighboring town. The Belice valley is known for their wines. Note: Very little wine was consumed as Sicilians drink the least wine per capita in Italy.

A few hours later (dinner time) the women began to assemble six pizzas in rectangular pans (Sicilian style), all with different toppings. Mushrooms, sausage, eggplant, porchetta were some of the toppings that I remember. The wood that was burning in the pizza oven all day was removed by the men, and all six pizzas were then cooked in the outdoor brick oven using only the retained heat. Again, the intense aromas permeated the air. I could not eat enough and enjoyed every bite. The women prepared the food and the men cooked it. The only item that the women cooked on the inside stove was the pasta.

All during that day different people came in and out. I believe we met about fifty, mostly relatives. The most important person that day was my great-aunt Laura Tardi (in Italy, women do not change their names when they get married). She was 94 at that time, mentally astute and just stopped driving the prior year. She is my grandmother's half-sister from my great grandfather's third marriage. This amazing woman was a wealth of information and answered most of my questions about my great grandfather's life. She mentioned that she was named after her father's first wife (my great grandmother) who died in America, due to complications of childbirth. One of Aunt Laura's daughters assisted with recording this vital information.

Peppino also called another one of my cousins who lives in Argentina. My great-grandfather's brother emigrated there around 1900. I spoke with him a bit, as my Spanish is much better than my Italian. We agreed to establish more communication upon my return home. I may even visit him in Argentina sometime in the future.

The gathering ended in the early evening. When I left, I was in an emotional state. My head was spinning. It seemed like a wonderful dream, not reality. I only believed it the next day when I woke up and verified it with my wife. The experience allowed me to increase my understanding of Sicilian family culture, taste authentic Sicilian food, meet relatives, and gather some important family history for the book *An Immigrant's Dilemma*. Another bonus was seeing how similar my family gatherings as a child were to this event.

This day I will never forget. Grazie mille, Peppino.

PART III

Our Language

""E perché il loro seggio regale (Federico II, Manfredi) era in Sicilia, è advenuto che tutto quello che i nostri precessori composero in volgare si kiama Siciliano; il che ritenemo anchora noi; et i posteri nostri non lo potranno mutare."

(And because their royal court (Frederick II, Manfredi) was in Sicily it happened that all that was composed in "volgare" is called Sicilian, which is what we still believe and our posterity cannot change that."

Dante Alighieri, *De Vulgari Eloquentia,* I-xii, p. 824.

Chapter 29

Sicilian and Italian Language Usage by Italian-Americans

Michael D. Pasquale, Ph.D.

When I was a child, I was surrounded by languages other than English, but in a faint and subtle way. My great-grandparents immigrated to Western New York in the late 1800s and early 1900s. They came from small towns in Sicily near Palermo and Messina, such as Valledolmo and Mazzarrà Sant'Andrea. I never met my great-grandparents, but I heard many stories. I was told that they mainly spoke Italian or what was called Sicilian "dialect."

These languages were only passed down in small phrases or isolated words. My grandparents, who were all born in western New York, never learned the language of their parents. The prevailing thought, strongly shared by many second-generation Italian immigrants, was that they only needed to use English since they were in America. This generation became what linguists call " passive bilinguals" in that they could understand the language spoken by their parents (a little) but could not actively use it beyond the isolated words or phrases. This tendency toward English was strong and within one generation most of the language was lost. However, words and phrases survived within the family and in their close-knit communities.

My parents were born after the war to Sicilian-American families. They both grew up in Western New York and were surrounded by cousins, aunts, and uncles. They were also part of a strong Italian community that shared a common culture and it demonstrated in the shared neighborhoods, grocery stores, and churches.

After the Vietnam War, as the baby boomer generation started families, many moved away from their extended families due to job opportunities or the desire to spread their wings beyond what they had always known. This was a drastic change from what Italian culture had been like, either in Europe or for the first few generations that settled in North America. My parents moved across the country, first for graduate school, and then for career, finally settling in Michigan. In Michigan we were far away from our immediate family and from the strong Italian community that my parents had grown up in. Therefore, the home that I grew up in was different from that which my parents had known. I only saw my grandparents a few times a year and my extended family of cousins only once a year when we took our annual pilgrimage back to New York for a few weeks every summer.

The language that surrounded my parents as they grew up lingered and showed up in a few areas in our home. Our Italian and Sicilian culture was important and that showed in our foods and customs. We valued ideas such as family, food, and faith. Now that I have my own family, I live near my parents and we have continued the practice of family dinner every Sunday after gathering for church service. I am also a university professor of linguistics (the study of language) and that interest has reignited the desire for me to not only learn more about the language of my family but also to pass it on to my siblings and children. Within the last few years, I was able to discover more about my family history in Sicily through the process of gaining dual Italian citizenship. Last year I was also able to trace my steps back to Sicily and visit my ancestral villages, the first time anyone in my immediate family had been to those villages in over 100 years.

So, what does my family remember of the languages spoken by my great-grandparents? I collected some words and phrases that I remembered hearing and interviewed my parents, aunts, and uncles about what they remember and have passed down.

A common memory is of a nursery rhyme recited by my great-grandmother and repeated by my grandmother and mother. However, my mother doesn't remember saying it to me, only to her doll when she was a girl. The internet is filled with recollections of Sicilian nursery rhymes that people remember hearing. However, many do not understand what they heard and in many cases it is like a game of "telephone" in which what is passed down is repeated in a slightly different way. I cannot find an example of the nursery rhyme in any other source that my relatives remember. This is what they remember (but no one knows what it means exactly):

Nina legga (?)
Porta pani

Mangia cu mia
(then tickle the baby at the end)

As I look through old nursery rhymes and Sicilian-English dictionaries I am unable to reconstruct what the original wording was. Clearly there is at least one line missing and the rhyme scheme is not observed. The only things clear are the last two lines: "Porta pani" means "brings bread" and "Papa" (for "father") could be a missing element. Other nursery rhymes have the idea of Papa coming and helping or bringing something for the baby. The last line clearly means "eat with me".

My relatives remember some other phrases that the older generation used among themselves or to children but were not in turn used by those new generations. These include the following:

Veni cà	"come here"
Ciao	"hi/good bye"
Baciami	"kiss me"

There were two other words that were remembered that were a bit inappropriate for the children to use, but they remembered hearing them.

Culo	"one's behind"
Buttana	"prostitute"

There were a few words and phrases that were used into the present day and the most common relate to food. It is interesting that some traditional Sicilian/Italian recipes in our family have only English names for them, such as the summer tomato and onion salad that we continue to enjoy. Also, some in the family use the English word for "artichoke" but others use the Italian word *carciofala*.

Here are some common words that our family still uses for Sicilian and Italian food:

Caponata	(eggplant relish)
Garduni	(burdock plant)
Cuccidati	(fig cookies)

It is interesting that my family pronounces the fig cookes, *cucci-dati*, with a "w" sound (e.g., "witch-adati").

Also desserts such as *cannoli* and *sfingi* (fried dough) are still commonly made at Easter and for St. Joseph's Day. It is interesting that the family uses these grammatically as English words and uses the English plural suffix –s (e.g., one cannoli, two cannolis, etc.) rather than the Italian usage of "one cannolo, two cannoli, one sfincia, two sfingi," etc.

There are other words that the younger generations remember hearing, but do not continue to use them. Some examples of these include various topics such as food, games, and other descriptive words.

Sugu	(tomato sauce)
Gumbari	(a friend or acquaintance)
Amerigani	(Americans, that is non-Italians)
Schifo	(something that is disgusting)
Acidu	(being sick to your stomach)
Cu Cu	(a Sicilian card game)
Dago	(derogatory term for a Sicilian or Italian)

As a linguist, I was interested in understanding the words used by my relatives. Sometimes this was difficult because words were passed down over the years by those not growing up speaking the language and using their memory. For example, for years our family made my grandmothers eggplant relish and called it "couplatina" (sounding like "couple of tina"). I remember being excited to figure out that they were referring to the Sicilian dish "caponata" (or the diminutive "caponatina"). I was also interested to see the possible influence of the Sicilian pronunciation of the "k" sound into the "g" sound (as linguists would refer to as "voicing"). This shows up in the words for *garduni* (from the word "cardone" also called "burdock" in English) and *gumbari* (from the Italian word "compare" and Sicilian word "cumpari" which is related to the Spanish word "compadre" meaning "friend or buddy"). The "k" to "g" sound also shows up in the word *amerigani* which means "American" or anyone who is not Italian. The 'r' in *gumbari* and *amerigani* are what linguists call 'flapped' sounds and are pronounced like a 'd.'

I remember my grandmother and my mother using the words

schifo "something disgusting" and *acidu* "being sick to your stomach." The word for tomato sauce that many relatives remembered was the word *sugu* (or some remember it pronounced as "suku"). Many times spaghetti with tomato sauce was referred to as "pasta sugu." As a child we often played the card game "Cuckoo", which I didn't realize until later was the Sicilian card game *Cu Cu.* Also, the first time I remember hearing the term *dago* was when my grandfather told me when I was a boy that I had permission to hit anyone who called me by that name. I had never heard myself called that before or since. It was an interesting glimpse into the history of my relatives who faced such persecution.

As I have tried to reconnect and reintroduce more Sicilian customs into our family, we continue to use words such as *garduni* and *caponata* (and explore recipes!). We have also introduced foods and recipes that are new to us such as *cassata, arancini*, and *pasta alla norma*, all of which we first tasted when we travelled to Italy.

As I raise my own sons, now the fifth generation since their great-great-grandparents immigrated from Sicily, I am not only learning to speak Italian, but I want to continue to remember words and phrases from our Sicilian family and hope that these continue to live on in our family.

Chapter 30

Sicilian Expressions

Excerpt from My First Two Dozen Years First appeared in *Arba Sicula XXXIV* (Recorded from **Memory)**

Anthony J. DeBlasi

Since I spoke Sicilian and English with equal fluency, I can and should comment on the difference between the two languages. Sicilian "feels" friendlier and warmer than English. On a cold-warm scale of 1 to 5, English is perhaps 2, while Sicilian is 5. Sicilian is more direct and earthy—at times brutally so—than English. I found that switching from English to Sicilian was like taking off a necktie or getting into more comfortable clothes. It cannot be emphasized too strongly that one language sees what another does not look at, enters places where another does not tread, and places value on things overlooked or ignored by another. Hence, the experience of one can never equal the experience of another, however skilled the translation.

NOTE

The spelling follows Italian rules of pronunciation. But:

j = English *y* [*j* is not used in Italian] *â* = two a's in a row *[a-a]*

It was a habit of the Trapanese to add *r* after *dd*, such that *beddu,* for example, was pronounced *beddru.*

(Other peculiarities of Sicilian pronunciation are omitted since they are not reflected in this list. ′ indicates accented syllable.)

FORMAT

The Sicilian phrase, in italics.

(A literal translation of the words, in parentheses.)

An English statement that suggests an equivalent thought, underlined.

An illustration showing the use of the Sicilian phrase.

The Expressions

A mmia metti manu? (You put hands on me?)

You should know better than to question [or test] my ability.

In a clothing shop, I would ask my mother if she could really afford to buy that high- priced coat for me, and she would say: A mmia metti manu?

A schifiu finiu. (It ended up ibadly.)

The situation has deteriorated [or it's gotten out of hand].

The price of food has gone up and papa would say: *A schifiu finiu.*

Chiss'è fissarìa. (That's a foolish thing.)

No big deal.

"You'll have to leave early to beat the shopping crowd before the holiday." *Chiss'è fissarìa.*

Chi ssemu priati. ("How pleased we are [with ourselves]!")

"Ain't we having fun!" [A sarcastic remark by one discovering illicit activity and ready to quash it.]

Kids are playing with "costumes" that are adult items of clothing, etc. from an off-limits closet. Enter an adult, catching them in the act: *Chi ssemu priati.*

Unn'u pigghiari ar'occhiu. (Don't take it by [steal it with] the eye.)

"Don't spoil it." [A verbal crossing of the fingers to keep a good thing safe or exclusive by not drawing attention to it.]

I report that a fig tree cutting seems to have rooted and showing signs of growth, and I get: *Unn 'u pigghiari ar'occhiu.*

Quannu ci pigghia, ci pigghia! (When it grabs, it grabs!)

What a damn thing!

A nail goes in crooked. The pliers disappear. The wood splits. Dad cries out: *Quannu ci pigghia, ci pigghia!*

Scurdarisi lu megghiu e lu chiù. (To forget the best and the most.)

To forget the most important thing.

You come home from shopping for all the things you need for holiday baking. When you discover that you forgot to buy sugar, you say: *Mi scurdai lu megghiu e lu chiù.*

Jetta lu sangu. (Shed [throw] blood.)
Serves him, [her, you] right [or Drop dead]!
"You're kidding! He'd have to rip up all the tiles he just laid, to straighten out that ripple." *Jetta lu sangu.*

Pigghiari pi fissa. (To take for a simpleton.)
Make a fool of [or treat as a patsy].
"After we agreed on the price for painting the outside of the house, I told the painter that if he wanted the job, he'd have to agree in writing to get his last one-third payment one month after he was finished. *Nuddru* [nobody] *mi pigghia pi fissa*"

Cu è fissa sta â so casa. (He who is a simpleton, let him stay in his own house.)
Using your head pays off.
You tell a friend that at the hardware store you found a tool with a minor defect, pointed that out to the manager, and got one-third knocked off the price, then add: *Cu è fissa sta â so casa.*

Mi fazzu fradiciu. (I make myself rotten.)
I just can't figure it (though I rack my brain).
Everything you've tried fails to get a simple thing to work [or you've thought of every possible explanation for some troublesome problem or anomaly]: *Mi fazzu fradiciu.*

'Na cosa di jornu. (A day thing.)
Get a move on.
Working on a repair, father asks son to fetch a tool, or find a certain size nail, etc., and the boy seems to take forever, and the father says: *'Na cosa di jornu.*

Attuppati l'aricchi. (Plug your ears.)
Have I got something to tell you [or Get a load of this]!
Before delivering some juicy gossip: *Attupati l'aricchi.*

Subbitu s'inn 'acchiana. (Right away he climbs up.)
He (she) blows a fuse.
I ask if he is telling the truth, and: *Subbitu s'inn'acchiana.*

S'un tingi, mascari'a. (If it doesn't stain, it soils.)

It may have missed the bull's eye but not the target [or Nothing ventured, nothing gained].

I contest a billing error over the phone and get no satisfaction, so I write a letter to the management. *S'un tingi, mascari'a.*

Ccà semu. (We're here.)

All we can do is wait and see.

A potentially serious storm has been predicted. "I wonder how bad it will be," someone says. The response: *Cca semu.*

Ci vulissi autru. (We should need something else.)

It's all we need. (Sarcasm for the opposite meaning.)

The husband says, "Don't worry. Business is picking up." The wife says: *Ci vulissi autru.*

Trascina facenni. (Dragger of business.)

Vagrant peddler of questionable business.

"A *trasci'na facenni* came to the door offering to replace the roof with something that would never have to be replaced again. I sent him away."

Pezzu di carni cu l'occhi. (Piece of meat with eyes.)

A dolt.

Advice to a lazy son or daughter: Get the lead out. Apply yourself and be somebody. Don't be a *pezzu di carni cu l'occhi.*

Ogni mali nun veni pi nociu. (Every evil does not come as a bother.)

A bad turn is sometimes a blessing in disguise.

You get fired and find a better job. *Ogni mali nun veni pi nociu.*

Affacciarisi quacchi fungia. (For some mushroom to appear.)

For something unforeseen to interfere.

You tell a friend that you got a buyer for your house and the deal looks good. He congratulates you and adds a note of caution: *Vidi ch'un t'affaccia quacchi fungia.* [Be ready for the unforeseen.]

Ci voli a conza di maiu. (It needs the repair of May.)

It needs major repair.

Said of anything that's going to take much time and effort to fix.

Tutti cacaru e ficeru a iddru. (Everybody defecated and made him.)

He thinks he's God's gift to the world.

Said of a conceited show-off, especially one who is no match for his boasts.

Fari lu malu sangu. (To make bad blood.)

To struggle [sometimes needlessly].

The furniture is rearranged, to make more room. Why *fari lu malu sangu?*

Ni voi si dici a li malati.

("You want some?" is asked of the sick [referring to food or drink.])

No need to ask—just give him (her) some.

Papa asks a visitor if he would like some wine. Mama says, *ni voi si dici a li malati.*

Quantu ci vulìa! (How much it needed!)

It's about time!

A package arrives that was expected much sooner: *Quandu ci vuli'a!*

Fa beni e scordatillu. Fa mali e pensacci. (Do good and forget it. Do evil and remember it.)

To sleep at night, do what's right.

One who gives a beggar money, giving the stranger the benefit of the doubt, might argue: *Fa beni e scordatillu. Fa mali e pensacci.*

Cariri comu u tumazzu nti maccarruna. (Falling like cheese on macaroni.)

A happy coincidence.

Shopping, you run into someone you needed to call, a circumstance that *carì comu u tumazzu ntii maccarruna.*

Un ti fari maravigghia. (Don't get yourself into [a state of] marvel.)

Don't think it can't happen to you.

A remark you make about someone's fall from grace has an air of superiority. You're told: *Un ti fari maravigghia.*

Cariri la facc'in terra. (For the face to fall on the floor (ground).)

Being terribly embarrassed.

The house was such a mess that it made *ca'riri la facc'in terra.*

Un'e dui e semu sempri drà. (One and two and we're always there [in the same place].)

Nothing ever changes.

An argument generates heat but solves nothing. *Un'e dui e semo sempri drà.*

U lupu perdi u pilu ma no u vizziu. (The wolf loses (sheds) his fur but not his vice.)

He (she) is, after all, the same person he (she) always was.

He said he was sorry and would quit doing it. But before long he started gambling again. *U lupu perdi u pilu ma no u vizziu.*

Putìa mancari? (Could it have missed?)

Just as expected.

A sore-loser shows up at a card game. *Puti'a mancari?*

Avìa vogghia. (It had will.)

No way (could it have been or worked out).

Giving up the search, someone later finds a dropped coin—oddly, on the other side of a door. Scratching his head, he says, *Avi'a vogghia truvarlu* (no w ay could I have found it).

Livari sta cuccagna. (To remove this abundance.)

It's time to end the party.

Mama hides the sweets from the raiders, saying, *Liva'mu sta cuccagna.*

a word typically used sarcastically . . .

abbuffati (Drink/eat your fill.)

[Commenting on a trifling amount, where more had been expected:] Have a feast!

The income tax refund computes to far less than anticipated. *Abbuffati.*

PART IV

Our Cuisine

"The most popular in the world"

Chapter 31

Italian-style Wedding Soup

Mario Toglia

One day at the National Archives on Houston Street I stopped to have coffee in their cafeteria. While I sat at the table thinking about the fast progress I had made with the passenger lists, I noticed the display board announcing the specials of the day. The first item that caught my attention was "*Italian-style wedding soup*. "What the heck is that?" I thought. I had never heard of a wedding soup, much less one that was Italian. I asked the concession worker for a description. He explained that it was a kind of chicken broth with small meatballs filled with spinach. It sounded something like what my mother used to prepare, only we called it "*brodo di acini 'e pepe*". The next day, surprisingly, I found the soup on the supermarket shelf. It was put out by Campbell's Soup, and by the picture on the can label, it did, indeed, look familiar. In fact, it brought to mind a time when my mother had made it one evening.

Now my father Ernest was in the manufacturing business. For years he made costume jewelry. But ever since he moved his factory from Spring Street, Manhattan to Brooklyn, he started manufacturing religious items like crosses and crucifixes. On this particular evening, my father showed up with a businessman just as my mother was setting the table. It was rare that my father would bring someone home to dinner, but usually there was some advanced notice - even if it were an hour. This time he hadn't even telephoned, and my mother was not the least bit happy. She lambasted him in their native dialect and the gist of her barrage was that if she had had advanced notice, she would have made something more palatable for "*lu 'Merigan*" - most likely steak and potatoes. But instead she had prepared a chicken broth soup with *acini di pepe* and small meatballs and the main dish was to be veal *pizzaiola*.

The visitor was also in the religious goods business and when he opened his mouth and spoke, I realized by his drawl that he definitely was not from our area, and was obviously from some far, remote part of the Deep South. I thought to myself that he probably had never met an Italian and most likely had never, never tasted Italian food in his life.

Now my mother always took pride in the foods that she prepared. They were always made fresh and from scratch. I remember how when she made *pasta lenticchia soup*, she would open up the bag of lentils and carefully separate the imperfect lentil from the good ones. Such soups as *acc' e patann, acc'e fasull', pasta fasull', minestra, cicoria, scarola, past' e cicera, brodo di acine 'e pepe* were common fare for us. These were the dishes that she had learned to make in her native Calitri with crops grown on the family's small patch of land outside town. By and large, these dishes would be labeled "peasant food." Among the myriad of recipes my mother knew, there were certain "peasant" dishes that she would serve "*in famiglia,*" due, perhaps, to the bitter taste of various greens or an unpleasant emanating odor. Then, of course, there were others that were prepared for "*gli altri.*" But regardless, the home cooked meals were always hearty and robust and nutritious.

As she placed the soup in front of our guest, I could see that she was anxiously awaiting his reaction. Would he like it or not? She apologized that she hadn't had advanced notice or she would have made something different. She told him that he didn't have to eat it if he didn't like it. Our guest fixed his eyes on the soup and pondered for awhile, seemingly wondering what those round balls were. He did admit that he had never had *Eye-tale-yin* food before.

I don't recall if our guest that evening had finished it or not, or whether he had enjoyed the veal *pizzaiola* and the green salad with mixed oil and red wine vinegar dressing, or my father's homemade wine. But I do recall the reaction of my non-Italian friends who had occasionally stayed at my house for dinner while working on some high school project. As one Irish schoolmate finally remarked after eating at my house a couple of times, "Gee, Mario, you eat the strangest looking food I have ever seen! I have never had anything like it before. And your mother's soup....... it was absolutely delicious!"

Italian-style wedding soup!?! The foods from Calitri don't need fancy name changes to be accepted on American tables. As my high school classmate concluded, "Calitrani food, it's m'm...m'm... good!"

This story is the author's remembrance which was included in his book, *They Came By Ship: The Stories of the Calitrani Immigrants in America*. The book, unique in theme, include over 100 stories written as a lasting tribute by descendants of immigrants from Calitri, Province of Avellino.

Chapter 32

It's the Food, Paisan'

Rosemary DeMaio Fariel

I was fortunate to have been raised in a large family where the kitchen was a central point and eating meals together was a part of our daily lives. Consequently, my most comforting memories are associated with food. Whenever I think of the days I spent with my mother while she prepared family meals, I feel her love and strong sense of family. The recollections are so clear and still linger in my mind of happy family gatherings around our dinner table. They will always remain a part of me and what I have become.

I was born in Dunmore, Pennsylvania. My parents, Giovanni and Vincenza Zarrilli DeMaio came from Calitri, Italy. I'm the youngest of eight children - first generation Italian-American but we were brought up Calitrani in many ways, particularly when it came to food.

I lived and grew up in an Italian section of Dunmore. My home was located on Chestnut Street where many other Calitrani families lived, such as the Zabattas, the Margottas and the Rubinos. I could visit the home of any *paisan* on almost any given day and discover the kitchen had the same cooking aroma as my own home. My mother's good friend Helen Margotta lived across the street and whenever I visited her, I'd find her cooking the same dish as my mother was preparing at home. And what was even more coincidental was the fact that the dishes would taste exactly the same!

This was pre-World War II era when food was home-grown and home cooked. Depending on the season, every home had a vegetable garden in the backyard. Meat was not in abundance and was added more as a flavoring. If vegetables were not grown in the back garden or received from one's neighbors, it meant they were purchased from the huckster who came around with his horse-drawn wagon. The huckster was always an Italian who sold vegetables preferred by the Italian palate. Perhaps the reason one could find the same meal in the neighborhood kitchens on any given day was because our mothers would buy the same produce from the same fruit-and-vegetable peddler. Our families even bought the same dairy products at the Ianelli Cheese Store at the end of the block. We knew that the mozzarella and the ricotta were always made fresh there each day.

Coming from a totally Italian neighborhood, I never saw a turnip, parsnip or rutabaga until I started my nurse's training in later years. I never knew the English word for *masanicol* or *prr'rr'zin* until I was at least 18 years old. Until I entered junior high - which was across town - my life experiences were very limited. Except for church and the elementary school which were in my neighborhood, my world was concentrated on one block.

In fact, in Dunmore the neighborhoods were defined by the aromas emanating from the kitchen windows. St. Mary's was the demarcation line between the Italian neighborhood and the "American" section. I can remember walking to the Junior High School in September when our homes - all the Italian homes - were preparing tomatoes for canning. My mother would buy several bushels of ripened tomatoes. I remember how I would dip the tomatoes in boiling water using a slotted spoon and, afterwards, peel the loosened skins off. My mother then put the tomatoes in canning jars for further seasoning or in a strainer to be crushed so that the juice would condense into tomato paste. The aroma of tomato paste and basil was in the air, but that disappeared once I walked through the American neighborhood. Here the scent was different. Here the mothers were making chili sauce and ketchup.

The schools in Dunmore did not have lunchrooms in those days. Each day, I had to return home to eat and I didn't have much time. My mother was always ready for me. If sandwiches were on the table, they were filled with freshly fried eggplants or roasted peppers and provolone cheese.

My mother prepared the meals the way she had learned in her native hometown. In Calitri there were no ovens in the homes; all the women would have their bread baked in the "community" ovens. For that reason, my mother usually cooked most of her meals on top of the stove. The only time she used the oven of our coal stove was to bake bread. On bread-baking days, a special treat called *pizza fritt'* was our breakfast meal. Later that day, the family would be served pizza

- her version - which was similar to focaccia bread. It was rectangular, topped with olive oil, salt, pepper, garlic, fresh herbs and sliced onions. My mother would do wonders with the leaf vegetables. She could turn dandelion leaves and other greens such as chicory, escarole, cabbage into an absolutely delicious *minestra*. Lentil soup and pasta fasull' were also a big part of our diet. At Christmas time I remember how the family would enjoy her honey covered struffoli balls and calzoni-shaped desserts filled with a sweet chocolate chestnut filling. It was called *cauzenciegghie*, and was a typical holiday treat from my parents' hometown.

My mother died in 1966, but fortunately there had always been an ongoing and loving relationship with our relatives in Calitri. Our relatives had come to visit us long before we had the opportunity to visit the hometown. It was in late summer 1999 when I had the opportunity to spend a few days with our relatives in Calitri. I had flown from Newark, New Jersey to Rome where I met up with my cousins, Vince and Jackie Zarrilli, and their daughter Christina. We rented a car and drove to Calitri. While Vince stayed in his father's house, I stayed with my cousin Lucia Cestone Zarrilli.

What a glorious five days! The celebrations were endless and the food was always the catalyst. However, one meal stands out from all the rest. It was suppertime and I was at the home of my cousin Canio Zarrilli. His wife Rosa was busy preparing the dinner. As she was cooking, an aroma filled the air that took me back to my home in Dunmore. She was preparing a simple meal - cavatelli with tomato sauce and spinach with garlic and oil. I was amazed at how much the food tasted exactly like my mother's. I remember sharing my nostalgic sentiments later that evening with my cousin, Vince. I turned to him and said in amazement,"I could swear my mother did the cooking."

Taken from the book *They Came By Ship: the Stories of the Calitrani Immigrants in America.*

Chapter 33

Acquasale

Mafalda LaCaruba Tornello

What can one do with hard bread, especially Italian bread that is more than three days old and is as solid as pumice rock? In my family we would grate it, add seasonings, and use the crumbs to bread cutlets and chops. However, in my husband's family, hard Italian bread would also be used for making a unique dish.

I had never heard of *acquasale* until I married into the Tornello family. Our families lived in North Tarrytown, a small ethnically mixed community on the Hudson River. Most families there knew one another, but I did not know this family until I met John Tornello at North Tarrytown High School. World War II had started and he immediately enlisted in the U.S. Navy and served on the Pacific Front. Upon his return, he finished his studies. We continued dating and later married in our small, lovely parish church on June 5, 1949. Once married, I became acquainted with another Southern Italian culture - similar to my Sicilian background, but distinctly unique. I also learned of their history and traditions.

John's parents were both from Calitri. His father Donato Tornello immigrated to New York in 1905. The surname had originally been Tornillo, but somewhere and somehow the spelling was changed to Tornello. In January of 1907, Donato sent for his parents Pasquale and Francesca Gautieri Tornello and his 12 year old sister Anna.

John's mother was Carmela Russo, daughter of Vincenzo and Francesca Ianuale Russo. She came to America in 1908, accompanied by her mother and younger brother Bernardino at the behest of her older married sister Lucia and her husband Michelarcangelo Russo who were then living in the Pocantico Hills section of North Tarrytown.

Donato and Carmela married on May 22, 1910 at St. Teresa of Avila Church in North Tarrytown. Papa Tornello then took his bride to New Rochelle where he labored at various jobs. Sometime about 1916, after the birth of their fourth child, they returned to North Tarrytown and Papa Tornello opened a small grocery store on Cortland Street. He would ride about 18 miles to the market in Yonkers by horse and wagon to buy produce by the bushel and groceries by the case. Later on, he would have a construction business. He was able to purchase a house at 35 Pocantico Street, North Tarrytown where his family grew in number. At that time my in-laws had eight children. One child Pasquale, though, died in 1928 at age 15. That same year, Papa Tornello opened a gas station on North Broadway next to the Tarry Diner. The following year John D. Rockefeller, Sr. purchased the Tornello house and other buildings in the square block area to build the Van Tassel Apartments. With the money, Papa Tornello bought a building lot in Webber Park in North Tarrytown where he built a large new home for his growing family. By 1930 there were nine children living at home: Angela, Francesca, Virginia, Donato Jr., Salvatore, Mary, John, Pasquale II and Lucille. With Papa Tornello working at the gas station, the job of caring for their family fell to my mother-in-law, Carmela.

In my opinion, my mother-in-law was a woman to be admired. With money being tight - especially during the Depression years - and with so many mouths to feed, Carmela was (from what I heard and observed) a very resourceful person. She had been raised in a very austere lifestyle. Her "waste nothing/use everything" approach came from her own experiences as a young girl in her native hometown. There in Calitri her family appreciated the little they had; here in America nothing was discarded that could be put to good use. Before the word "recycle" came into being, my mother-in-law was already re-using the large 12-½ inch metal lids that capped empty commercial-sized shortening cans as her cake baking tins. Indeed, the cakes she baked were always three-layered and delicious. From what I have tasted from her kitchen, I can truly say she was an excellent cook.

In fact, my introduction to Mamma Tornello's kitchen was an eye-opener. With such a large family, the preparation of family meals had to be demanding and overwhelming. In her pantry hung an assortment of pots and pans, the size of which I had never seen. Yet, she handled the oversized pasta pot, colander, cake pans and frying pans with ease as she lovingly prepared the meals for her family. For most people this would have been comparable to preparing a holiday banquet, but somehow this ordinary woman managed to do it every day. For dinner, she would even prepare several dishes to please the diverse palate of family members. The roasts she baked were always surrounded by lots of potatoes and onions, seasoned to a mouth-watering perfection. On Sundays, a clean sheet was placed over one of the beds, ready to accept the hundreds of ravioli she so ably made from scratch. And her homemade breads! How everyone loved to dunk her fresh bread into a bowl of her *minestra* or *pasta fasull'* in order to soak up the delicious soup. There was no such thing as leftovers. The food would be re-heated and eaten at another time. And as for bread that might become hard...well, it would be "recycled" into a Calitran dish called *acquasale.*

I will never forget the first time I experienced this traditional Calitran dish. It was a Sunday at the Tornello house, at a time when most of the family lived in close proximity and grandchildren were not yet a celebrated addition. We had all enjoyed Mamma's homemade ravioli, roast chicken and salad around one o'clock. Later, some of the men gathered in the living room before the TV set; some went for a stroll around the neighborhood. The women cleared the dining table and kept busy in the kitchen while chatting amiably, joking and discussing family matters. As was custom, the large dining table was a favorite place to gather. As evening approached my sister-in-law Frances asked if we were hungry. No one was enthusiastic in responding, but suddenly someone said, "You know, I'm not really hungry, but I could go for some acquasale." I remember thinking, "*Acquasale? Isn't that salty water?*" Well, of course, once everyone heard "acquasale" they thought it was a terrific idea and a great way to end the Sunday at Mamma's. I joined some of the family in the kitchen and watched as they prepared the dish. When the steaming plates of acquasale were set on the table it was as though a banquet had been prepared for the royal family. At first I was a little reluctant to try, but with a little coaxing I dug in.

So many years have gone by since my introduction to acquasale, but from what I have noticed the appeal was very strong for the many Calitrani-Americans who lived in the Tarrytown area. They would make it whenever the occasion necessitated a quick meal - and it certainly was served a lot during those meatless Fridays.

I don't eat acquasale that often anymore, but when I do I always remember Mamma and the happy days in her kitchen. Mamma

Tornello died on October 1, 1956 at the age of 68. She left behind a legacy of hard work, devotion to one's family, the art of living simply and honestly, and the joy of cooking for family and friends. To this day, I never throw away leftover Italian bread. When the yen strikes my husband John, I will hear him bustling about the kitchen and I immediately know that he is preparing a favorite dish – acquasale.

Recipe for making Acquasale

- A slab of good Italian bread which has hardened
- Approximately 2 cups of water
- 1 or 2 large or jumbo eggs
- 3 tablespoon of olive oil
- 1 clove of garlic salt and red pepper to taste

Place bread in a soup dish and set aside Bring water to a boil in a small saucepan. Crack egg(s) into water to poach. Cook approximately 1 minute or less. Yolk should not be poached dry. Carefully pour only the boiling water over the bread, gently setting the egg(s) aside. In a small frying pan, add the oil and a peeled clove of garlic. Cook only until the garlic turns a golden brown.

Discard the garlic. Season oil with salt and red pepper, being careful pepper does not brown. Place an empty soup dish right side up on top of the bread soaking in the soup dish that had been set aside. Press together, squeezing out the excess water from the bread. Gently place the egg(s) on top of the bread. Pour the seasoned oil on top of the egg(s). Eat while it is hot.

Taken from They Came By Ship: The Stories of the Calitrani Immigrants in America, *Xlibris Publishers.*

PART V

On Being Sicilian

"One of the first character traits that is most evident to outsiders is the great pride that Sicilians have in themselves and in their homeland. It is significant that Sicilians, especially those who live in a foreign country, will go out of their way to tell you how proud they are of being Sicilian."

Reprinted by permission from the book: *What Makes a Sicilian?*, Gaetano Cipolla, Legas, 1996

Chapter 34

"Picchí Semu Siciliani"

Nino Provenzano

Me figghia, c'avi attornu a li deci anni,
e va a la scola quinta elementari,
spissu mi 'nqueta facennu dumanni
di cosi chi la stannu a 'nteressari.
Lu patri è di duviri, comu granni
di dari spiegazioni onesti e chiari.
Ma a li voti, cririti, è na gran cruci.
Di spiegazioni va finisci a vuci.

L'autra sira mi dissi: "Papà,
l'essiri Siciliani chi vol diri?"
"Ma comu, figghia mia, eu e la mamà
vinnimu di 'nSicilia, l'ha sapiri.
Tu e li to soru nascistivu ccà,
Siculi-Americani a un finiri
Ma cu è ccà dintra Sicilianu parra
e a cu 'un ci piaci è 'mpintu pi na garra.

Nun criu chi ti dispiaci chista storia,
d' essiri Siciliana discinnenti,
o a chista età ti muntasti di boria
e di l'eredità 'un capisci nenti?"
"Ma no, papà, lu sacciu già a mimoria;
li cosi chi m'hai a diri l'haiu a menti.
Archimedi, Bellini e Vanni Meli
La scienza e l'arti purtaru a li celi

"Ma 'un'è sulu picchissu, figghia mia,
chi t'ha vantari chi si Siciliana.

Chapter 34

"Why We Are Sicilians"

Nino Provenzano
Translated by Gaetano Cipolla

My daughter who's about ten years of age,
and who is in fifth grade in elementary school
often will pester me with many questions
about the things which she finds interesting.
I feel that as the father I must try
to offer explanations that are clear
and honest, but believe me, on occasions,
we go from explanations to a fight.

The other night, she said to me, "Say, Dad,
What does it mean that we are Sicilians?"
"Whatever do you mean, my child? You know
that both your mother and myself came here
from Sicily. You and your sisters were born here,
you are both Sicilian-Americans,
but in this house Sicilian's what we speak.
If someone doesn't like it, it's too bad!

I don't believe that you will have objection
to being the offspring of two Sicilians
or is it that your head is swollen so
you don't know anything about our heritage?"
"No, Dad! I know that story all by heart.
The things you're going to tell me now I know:
Archimedes, Bellini, Meli were great lights
who science, music, art brought to the heights."

"But that is not the only thing, my child* ,
that ought to make you proud to be Sicilian.

Nui semu razza d'antica valia,
amamu cosi boni e vita sana.
Nui semu sempi amanti d'allegria,
di l'eleganza e la vita baggiana.
Ditistamu la vita sulitaria
c'un fa pi nui e certamenti è laria.

Amamu la natura, lu campari,
semu aguriusi e assai granni di cori.
Forsi nun semu ricchi di dinari,
ma canuscemu autri tisori.
La cucina paisana fa scialari,
cu la canusci, l'ama e sinni gori.
Pi gusti nui vantamu lu dirittu
chi sudisfari fa ogni pitittu.

'Mmagina un munnu senza li spaghetti,
o la lasagna, li ziti 'nfurnati,
dda ricca sarsa chi 'ncapu ci metti,
li ficu sicchi e l'alivi salati.
La capunata, stigghiola purpetti,
cannola, cassateddi, li cassati.
Si eu 'un nascia 'nSicilia, Diu ni scanza,
ma cu la cunurtassi sta me panza?"

We are an ancient, worthy race of people.
We love good things and live a healthy life.
We love to be surrounded by good cheer,
by elegance, a life that's full of joy;
we cannot stand a life of solitude.
It's boring and against our disposition.

We love the countryside, we love to live,
we're curious and very generous as well
Maybe we are not rich in terms of money,
but other treasures we can understand:
Italian cooking gives our heart much joy.
Whoever knows it loves it and enjoys it.
As far as flavors go, we're glad to boast
that we can satisfy each person's taste.

Imagine then a world without spaghetti,
lasagna, baked ziti, with that savory sauce!
We love our dried figs, salted olives,
caponata, stigghioli, meatballs,
and stuffed eggplants! Desserts, like cannoli,
sweet cakes, cassata and almond cookies!
If I had not been born in Sicily,
what joy would my poor stomach offer me?"

Chapter 35

Parting Words

Mark Hehl

North America is a bastion of immigrants (my wife is an immigrant). Except for those of Native American ancestry, we all can trace our heritage back to somewhere else, whether our ancestors came on the Mayflower or a slave ship, into Ellis Island, JFK Airport or across the Rio Grande. Our immigrant ancestors blessed this continent with varied cuisines, customs, and traditions, while bringing their strong family values. Yearning for freedom and opportunity, they fought to overcome ignorance, bigotry, and prejudice. While being abused and exploited, these various nationalities worked to build this continent. Future generations have benefitted from their sacrifices.

I believe that we owe it to their memory to maintain and pass down these family traditions no matter where they emigrated from. It is my wish that others work to document their traditions and heritage, whatever they are.

Other Books by Contributors:

Joseph L. Cacibauda, *After Laughing Comes Crying: Sicilian Immigrants on Louisiana Plantations*, Mineola, NY, Legas, 2009

Joseph L. Cacibauda, *Not For Self: A Sicilian Life and Death in Marion*, Mineola, NY, Legas, 2017

Louisa Calio, *In the Eye of Balance*, Ridgefield, UT, Paradiso Press, 1978

Louisa Calio, *Journey to the Heart Waters*, Mineola, NY, Legas, 2014

Angelo F. Coniglio, *The Lady of the Wheel (La Ruotaia)*, Mineola, NY, Legas, 2012-2019

Gaetano Cipolla, *What Makes a Sicilian?*, Mineola, NY, Legas, 1996-2001

Anthony J. DeBlasi, *Korea -- Back when . . . .* , Montgomery, AL, E-BookTime, 2007-2017*

Anthony J. DeBlasi, *Nine Pieces for Heart and Mind*, Montgomery, AL, E-BookTime, 2006*

Marisa Frasca, *Via Incanto: Poems from the Darkroom*, New York, NY, Bordighera Press, 2014

Marisa Frasca, *Wild Fennel: Poems and Other Stories*, New York, NY, Bordighera Press, 2019

Mark Hehl, *Amusing Confessions of an International Consultant*, Woodbury, CT, Mark Hehl, 2017

Mark Hehl, *An Immigrant's Dilemma*, Mineola, NY: Legas, 2019.

Betsy Vincent Hoffman, *Dreaming of Sicily A Travel Memoir*, New Market, MD, Betsy Vincent Hoffman, 2009

Mario Toglia, *Celebrating the Heritage*, Bloomington, IN, Xlibris Publishers, 2015

Mario Toglia, *Preserving Our History*, Bloomington, IN, Xlibris Publishers, 2013

Mario Toglia, *THEY CAME BY SHIP: The Stories of the Calitrani Immigrants in America,* Bloomington, IN, Xlibris Publishers, 2007

Alfred Zappala, *The Reverse Immigrant*, Mineola, NY, Legas, 2010

Alfred Zappala, *Gaetano's Trunk*, Mineola, NY, Legas, 2011

Alfred Zappala, *Figghiu Beddu*, Mineola, NY, Legas, 2013

Alfred Zappala, *Joy of My Heart,* Mineola, NY, Legas, 2015

*These books are out of print: Contact tonyjdb@metrocast.net for electronic copies

About the Editor and Author

Mark Hehl is an engineer, consultant, and public speaker. He is the author of the books *An Immigrant's Dilemma* and *Amusing Confessions of an International Consultant*. Mark is a keynote speaker at various worldwide locations and has been a frequent guest on national public radio. He is the son of a Sicilian-American mother and spent his early years around his Sicilian relatives.